THE LOST JEWS

Last of the Ethiopian Falashas

Louis Rapoport

STEIN AND DAY/*Publishers*/**New York**

For my father, and for Sylvia, Ehud and Adi

Rapoport, Louis.
    The lost Jews.

    Bibliography: p. 233.
    Includes index.
    1. Falashas—History.   2. Ethiopia—Ethnic relations.
3. Israel—Emigration and immigration.
I. Title.
DS135.E75R27   963'.004924   79–92340

ISBN 0–8128–2720–1

Acknowledgments

I wish to thank especially Sol Stern for his invaluable insight and suggestions. Thanks also to Meyer Levin, Prof. Wolf Leslau, Prof. John A. Williams, Prof. Howard Lenhoff, Graenum Berger, Nate Shapiro, Michelle Schoenberger, Jim Quirin and Prof. Robert Hess. This book obviously depended on the cooperation of members of the Beta-Israel tribe. Most of the Falasha names—and two names of Israelis—in the book are pseudonyms, particularly in the chapters dealing with the tribe's current situation.

Contents

Foreword by Meyer Levin

It must have been in the twenties, at college, that I read a magazine article about a tribe of black Jews in Ethiopia, called the Falashas, whose origins were almost mythological, dating back to Biblical times. The magazine must have been the *Menorah Journal,* predecessor of *Commentary*, and the article must have been connected with the re-re-re-discovery of the tribe, for the discoveries took place every few centuries, culminating in our time in the studies of the Falasha culture by the French-Jewish scholar, Prof. Jacques Faitlovitch.

There is a phrase in Hebrew, *meshuga l'davar,* which might be translated as "crazy on the subject," but which has a somewhat deeper connotation, for the subject usually has the element of a cause. The Falashas are today a cause, a cause that activates hundreds of persons in various organizations and committees in the United States, Europe, and Israel.

Louis Rapoport, while an editor on the *Jerusalem Post,* became *meshuga l' davar* as to the Falashas, and then spent years writing this book. Rapoport has written a stirring, thoroughly researched book on this almost lost phenomenon, a book which should stimulate a last-chance rescue of this most ancient of Jewish communities. It is a passionate work which traces and exposes the intrigues, the high-level indifference and even sabotage that has impeded the rescue effort. Jewish world institutions, and Israeli institutions, and the world's non-particularistic rescue organizations seem unable or disinclined to save this endangered people, to do more than stand by and watch the disaster that is occurring.

True, there is controversy on this point. Some say scandal. There are pro-Falasha organizations in England and the United States that have been active since the days of Prof. Faitlovitch in sending aid to the Falashas: health aid, educational aid, economic aid, but based on the principle of keeping the community intact in its Ethiopian environment. During this half-century the result has been a population dwindled to half, and now threatened with extinction. On the other side are those who insist that the remaining twenty-eight thousand Falashas must be moved en masse to Israel, as were the Yemenite tribes.

Over ten years ago I was able to carry out my own *meshugas* on the subject, when El Al initiated a weekly flight to Addis Ababa. Two of my friends were sent as television reporters—Larry Frisch and Lazar Bianco—and I persuaded them to stay on and go with me to the Falasha villages near Gondar, the ancient Ethiopian capital where, many centuries ago, a Falasha queen ruled. For at their height, the Falashas numbered a million. But all this will be found in fascinating detail in Louis Rapoport's book, which combines deep research with vivid present-day reporting. His book is journalism at its best—imbued with a cause and yet objective, fully informed, fearless.

On our own trip to northwest Ethiopia, we succeeded in making a half-hour film of the Falasha way of life in the village of Ambover. What surprised me was that the images proved more Biblical than African.

As it happened, our film became part of the re-awakening of interest in the Falashas. But most arousing are the political events that, during this decade, increasingly threaten to bring an end to what is the oldest continuously existent Jewish community on earth. As Louis Rapoport describes, the Falashas, having survived oppression, epidemics, destitution, and proselytization, are now under attack by organized brigands who capture the despised Jews, the "witch-people," in remote villages, and sell them into slavery. Thousands of Falashas, forced to give up their identity, are among the half-million Ethiopian refugees who have fled over the borders in the violent upheavals of the last several years.

The Falasha cause means not only the saving of a very special culture, but also of a people, a wonderful people, beautiful, patient, diligent, devoted, imbued with their centuries-long sense of continuation. May every reader of this book become *meshuga l' davar*.

The Lost Jews

1

A Falasha Message

"Our people here entered into cold and into sleep, a very strong sleep. We are still waiting with much patience and hopes to our salvation by the Israeli nation in our holy country for which we are dreaming . . . A few months ago, I wrote to you and you didn't answer to my letter. Haim, you have to think about the students, about the boys, the girls who are getting killed for many reasons. Is there any way to save their lives? Before they are all killed and nobody will remain? I think that our days will not be long anymore, but I am asking you to at least take care of our families, our children our small children."

The Ethiopian Jew who wrote that letter was imprisoned as a "Zionist agent" two months after he sent his desperate plea to an Israeli. In a second letter, his last as a free man, the Falasha religious teacher, a sensitive young man whose mother interpreted dreams in their village in remote northwest Ethiopia, wrote again to the Israeli, who was helping to conduct a lukewarm effort to save the Ethiopian Jews: "We will not sell our souls, to lose our faith and our traditions. We will repeat again and again until maybe only one man will remain to tell the story and to ask for help, emergency help, to save a whole nation, a whole tribe, who was dedicated for a thousand years to his faith beyond the dark mountains of Ethiopia."

The Falashas' enemies spent hundreds of years whittling down Ethiopia's indigenous people, the Agaw, to whom the Falashas are related. The Jewish tribe that numbered perhaps one million was gradually reduced to twenty-eight thousand terrified survivors in a slow genocide waged first with spears and then with guns in the rugged highlands. In recent years there has been a resurgence of large-scale killing in northern Ethiopia, where rebel armies and bandit gangs roam the countryside. And the Falashas, or Beta-Israel as they call themselves, faced brutal *shiftas* (bandits)—Cossacks of the Great Rift mountains; left-wing insurgents, and mercenaries hired by right-wing feudal landlords, who had been deposed by the Marxist regime.

But the remnant of what Israel's chief rabbis call the lost tribe of Dan might be better off if they were the whales, wog turtles or seal pups that tug at so many hearts. It is an age when a segment of humanity can be destroyed with virtual impunity. And when a leader of the small Falasha community in Israel came to America in the spring of 1979 to try to raise support for his tribe, he began to realize the indifference of even coreligionists, the American Jews.

Asa Azariah was a true exotic on display in the million-dollar Pacific Heights mansion of a San Francisco family. People had gathered for an evening "featuring the only Falasha in the United States," according to the flier sent out

by the local American Jewish Congress. It called him a
representative of "what some rabbinical authorities call one
of the Lost Tribes of Israel . . . Said to be direct descendants of King Solomon and Queen of Sheba . . ."

Asa, a slight, handsome man whose brown face is dominated by the large round eyes that set Ethiopians apart from
other Africans, had lived in Israel for ten years, served as a
sergeant in the Golan Heights, and studied history at Tel
Aviv University. Now, he had come for a two-month tour of
America, paid for by a Jewish student group and the American support committee for the Falashas, to talk to some
small gatherings like this one and to communicate some
vital news about his people, the black African Jews.

Asa Azariah swallowed the first words of his speech—
he seemed shy and unaccustomed to talking to more than a
few persons at a time and there were forty crowded into the
salon, trying to follow his halting English. "Louder,
please," someone spoke up. They sat on luxurious sofas and
stuffed chairs, on the Oriental rugs and on the bench of the
ebony Steinway grand. An Israeli-American helped Asa to
translate unfamiliar words from Hebrew to English: "genocide," "slavery," "corruption." The guests were mostly
middle-class professionals who had heard something or other
about the Falashas. Some of the guests had come to see the
curious phenomenon of an African whose ancient people
believed that they were the only Jews left alive in the
world—up until the tribe was "rediscovered" by European
Jews a century ago. Disbelief registered on several faces.

"He doesn't look Jewish," one woman in her seventies
confided to her neighbor. Pointing at the translator, she

asked: "What language are they speaking?" Most Jews wouldn't catch the difference between Hebrew and Tagalog, so it was not a surprising question. It would never occur to the woman that this African might know far more about Jews and Israel than she did—but then, it's not always easy for American Jews to accept the fact that "their" Israel is composed of a majority of Jews from Asian and African countries; that the dark, more "primitive" Jews outnumber the Ashkenazim from Russia and Poland, South America, and the English-speaking countries.

Asa sketched the Falashas' rich history for his audience, telling the story of Falasha Queen Yehudit, who had conquered a vast empire in the tenth century, dealt a devastating blow to Christianity, and changed the course of Ethiopian history. He described the centuries-long conflict with the Christians, the defeat of the Falashas and the scattering of the tribe. Everyone tried to listen, straining to hear Asa's faltering, monotonous voice. "He has no oomph," one of the sponsors of the talk whispered, disappointed. But when Asa brought the story up to date and described the events happening to his tribe, interest perked up—for it was turning into a horror story:

"In 1975 the Israeli government was willing to give the Law of Return to the Falashas . . . the news reached Ethiopia and the Falashas were so happy and didn't want to lose time . . . and they sold their belongings and came down from the mountain villages to wait for the first planes to come and take them to Israel. But unfortunately," Asa said quietly, drawing out his words, "at this time it did not happen. A new military government came to power, Marxists, and made the land reform, giving the Falashas freedom to own land for the first time, and to be treated as equals with the Christians. This land reform angered the Christian aristocrats of the old regime who still had private armies.

"They hated the Falashas, who had for long been their servants . . . The new government of Ethiopia didn't have enough power in the area where the Falashas are living"; and the number of massacres kept growing in 1977 and especially 1978. Many villages were totally destroyed. Jewish people were killed in big numbers, sold in marketplaces in different regions in Ethiopia and sold in Sudan.

"When the news of the tragedy in Ethiopia reached the children who are living in Israel, we made big efforts for two years, and we brought these matters before different organizations, including the ministers of Israel . . . But during this time, we were told they would take care of the Jews in Ethiopia. But nothing was done. There were thousands of Falasha refugees who were suffering without food or shelter and without getting any help neither from the Jews nor the Ethiopian government . . . seven thousand refugees up to now are hoping for help from the Jewish organizations and the Jewish world. The situation in Ethiopia today is disaster; I would say, almost a holocaust."

There were concentration camp survivors in the room, others who had fled after *Kristallnacht*. And those who had witnessed the Nazi nightmare took Asa at his word. A wealthy woman with silver hair and a hawk-like face stared intently at him, trying to detect a trace of what she conceived of as "Jewishness," battling with her conscience about whether to get involved.

Asa, standing with his arms behind his back next to a huge oil portrait of the lady of the house, repeated his muted cry to the Jewish world: "Thousands of Falashas are being killed or sold into slavery." And he reminded the people in the room of the time when six million Jews were destroyed; when the American Jewish establishment during World War II was silent about first reports of the Holocaust, and the fact that two million Jews had been murdered rated a five-inch story on page six of the *Washington Post* . . .

Asa Azariah alluded to other parts of the story: How some Israeli officials had either blocked the Falashas' rescue or pooh-poohed their warnings until it was too late. How Minister of the Interior Yosef Burg had likened the Falashas to "Martians" and dismissed their claim to being Jews. How Moshe Dayan had inadvertently caused a pogrom with a "slip of the tongue." How Abba Eban, who is esteemed as a Hebrew demigod by American Jews, had dismissed the pleas of the Falashas during and after his years as foreign minister, terming the destiny of the Beta-Israel "a marginal problem."

Asa suppressed his fury as he talked to his first audience of American Jews—there was no point in offending their ignorance with too much of the truth. But it was important to make it clear that world Jewry could have done something, and still could, that these supporters of Israel Bonds should take more interest in how their money was being used to build Israel, to save Soviet Jews and Syrian Jews, Iranian and Argentinian Jews. In contrast, nothing of consequence had been spent to rescue black Jews who were saying that they faced immediate slaughter.

The half-hearted efforts of Israel and world Jewish organizations to save the Falashas soured several supporters of the tribe in Israel and America. They saw years of broken promises, of news censored in the name of "quiet diplomacy," condescending dismissals of the seriousness of the tribe's plight by cynical politicians, organization professionals and bureaucrats with the power of life and death in their hands. In the end, the Beta-Israel were crying out that they were being betrayed, that even well-intentioned people in the Israeli government and executives in organizations like World ORT Union had contributed to the extinction of Ethiopia's Jews.

Before 1977, Israeli officials had been totally skeptical of reports that the Falashas were facing slaughter. "It's just a ploy," was the opinion expressed by former envoys to Ethiopia, officials in the Jewish Agency, executives of the Interior Ministry and the Foreign Ministry, politicians in the religious establishment and Ethiopia experts at the university. Underlying it all was a certain basic attitude: "Look, don't we have enough problems, what do we need these *schvartzes* for?" It was the sentiment—and sometimes the words used in private—behind Israel's tepid effort to help the embattled tribe. It was in marked contrast to the campaigns waged on behalf of Syrian Jewry—which became a political football—or the big secret effort to rescue Iranian Jews when the shah fell. The huge campaign to coax a handful of comfortable American Jews to immigrate to Israel amounts to tens of millions of dollars. The budget to save twenty-eight thousand people has been minuscule in comparison. A set of financial priorities in immigration is obviously necessary in a country like Israel, which has absorbed refugees and immigrants from ninety countries. There's a special category for the endangered Jewish communities—a subject that is censorable in Israel, often for good reason. There's no question that thousands of Jewish lives are at stake in Communist Russia, in fascistic Argentina, in mullah-ruled Iran, in Syrian ghettoes. But the Falashas of Ethiopia have always been at the bottom of the immigration ladder. Beleaguered Israel needs educated people, not more *primitives,* the argument goes.

Many Israelis recognize that the country's biggest internal Jewish problem is the schism of the two Israels: the children of the Ashkenazim—Jews of Europe—and the Oriental-Sephardi Jews of Asia, southern Europe and Africa. It is "Second Israel," the Oriental Jews, that pushed for recognition of the Ethiopian Falashas as Jews entitled to immigrate to Israel. And it was the Sephardis' chief rabbi, Ovadia Yosef, who had proclaimed in 1972 that the Falashas were of the seed of Dan, the tribe whose greatest son was Samson, that they were Jews who must be brought back to their ancestral home, Israel—it was a divine imperative, the rabbi declared.

The three hundred Falashas who had come to Israel singly or in small groups over a period of thirty years exulted in the chief rabbi's epic ruling, which was based on the findings of other great rabbis. But the Falashas' hopes would be crushed: they would suffer years of empty promises, ham-handed rescue attempts and the smug complacency of officialdom.

By 1979 the Israeli Falashas broke their long silence to protest against the handling of the tribe's fate. They couldn't be accused of "unpatriotic" motives—although there are some people who think that any criticism of Israel is disloyal and feeds anti-Semitism. Asa Azariah and other Beta-Israel leaders believed that some officials had acted criminally, and *intentionally*—for their inaction had caused disasters. The Falashas also thought that other bureaucrats *inadvertently* had contributed to the damage.

In 1977, Prime Minister Menachem Begin—the first Israeli leader ever to meet with the Israeli Falashas—told them he would help the Falashas, and he advised them to continue to "keep quiet." But apparently he didn't tell Moshe Dayan, then Israel's foreign minister. In February, 1978, Dayan told a press conference in Geneva that Israel was helping to arm Ethiopia against its enemies, an announcement that shut the door on Falasha emigration and sparked a bloody rightist pogrom against the tribe: The landlord-led EDU (Ethiopian Democratic Union) rebels, infuriated that Israeli arms were being used against their forces, went on a rampage against the Beta-Israel "Zionists" and destroyed whole villages. Babies were bludgeoned to death, children's feet were hacked off, men were killed or castrated, women were raped and mutilated, old people were left tied to thorny bushes, their slashed skin drying and cracking in the sun. Captives were sold in the slave trade that still thrives in Ethiopia and the Horn of Africa. The Geneva-based ORT organization in a 1978 report said that slave raids were directed against the Falashas of Woggera around Dabat, a region the Ethiopian Democratic Union had occupied for several months. One Falasha blacksmith fetched seven hundred *birr*, about $350. And the Falashas were also the target of another rebel army, the leftist EPRP (Ethiopian Peoples Revolutionary Party). The reasons were the same: "Zionist" Ethiopians were characterized as the arch enemy. When Falashas refused to join the leftist insurrection, they were murdered. And the Falashas feared that even the central government, to which they remained loyal, might be turned against them.

In 1978, hundreds, perhaps thousands, of Falashas were routed from their village homes, and they streamed into the area around the town of Gondar, Ethiopia's former capital. The displaced tribespeople sold whatever meager possessions remained and waited in messianic expectation for a rescue plane to take them to Israel.

The only thread connecting the Falashas to their core-ligionists was ORT, a Jewish organization that some Falashas thought was contributing to the tribe's destruction. World ORT Union started its development program in Falasha country in 1976; and its $2 million budget for Ethiopia depended on grants from the American, Canadian, German, Swiss and Dutch governments, not on any funds from Jewish organizations. To qualify for the grants, the program had to be nonsectarian and of benefit to the entire province, in which the Falashas are less than one percent of the population.

In early 1979, the Israeli citizen who headed ORT's program in Gondar claimed that ORT was "contributing to the destruction of the tribe"; he said there were seven thousand Falasha refugees in the area, not the one thousand to two thousand ORT officials in Geneva claimed. And he charged that a Christian Ethiopian employee of ORT had a role in the execution of a fellow employee, who was a Falasha, and in the arrest and torture of several religious teachers. The Israeli, an ex-kibbutznik—call him Amos Ozari—also alleged that there was mismanagement of funds; specifically, that of $200,000 that had reportedly been distributed as loans to Falasha farmers, only $1,490 had actually been received. Other ORT employees, past and present, supported some of Ozari's claims. Two ORT employees in Geneva said privately they believed "private fortunes were being made" on the black market. Two Swiss potters hired by ORT to work in Gondar also protested against their employer, saying that ORT personnel mistreated the Falashas. The American Committee for the Falashas drew up a list of twenty two charges, demanding an answer from the American ORT organization and World ORT in Geneva.

For months, the Ozari allegations created a storm among several major Jewish organizations and set off informal inquiries in Israel and by representatives of the countries contributing to the development fund, including USAID. Worried ORT officials brought several visitors to see for themselves. British publisher David Kessler went to Gondar in June of 1979 and claimed that all of the charges were nothing but lies. He said the Falashas "adore" ORT's development director, the main target of Ozari's charges. Kessler said the Falashas were greatly benefiting from ORT's projects, and his evaluation was backed up in July by two USAID representatives and a Canadian aid official who also visited the ORT projects. The USAID people reported that the security situation in the area was vastly improved, although attacks were still continuing in the Aramcho Valley, from where displaced Christians as well as Falashas were fleeing to Gondar. They said that there were no more than one thousand Falasha refugees and added that the tribe's situation had generally improved with the help of ORT agriculture and construction projects. Local Ethiopian authorities were tolerant of religious freedom for the Falashas, the Westerners reported, and the government had ordered the market in Gondar to be open on Sundays so the Falashas would no longer be forced to violate their religion by selling their wares—pottery, weavings, and metal goods—on Saturdays. An unofficial Israeli commission of inquiry also rejected Ozari's charges.

The response by several Falashas and some of their American supporters was that a criminal cover-up had been perpetrated, that each of the investigating parties had its own interests to advance and that the big Jewish organizations had simply rallied behind "one of their own" for fear that their own financial records might be subjected to investigation. But there was no substantiation of the charges, no hard evidence of any kind, although an audit of ORT's books in Geneva was still pending.

The situation had become extremely complex, making any objective assessment difficult. The Falashas' obsession about Israel and their general desperation has thousands of years of history behind it, and fact and fiction were sometimes blurred. Their lives have been hanging in a delicate balance; and the signals emitting from an endangered species are sometimes obscured . . . But for the Falashas in Israel, agonizing over the fate of their families, it was crystal clear: One of them received a letter saying seven members of his family had been killed. Another Israeli Falasha lost his parents and two brothers, and so it went.

One impassioned letter, composed by a religious teacher who had once lived on an Israeli kibbutz, insisted that the danger of annihilation was never greater: The EPRP and EDU were trying to incite a government pogrom:

June 20, 1978

We have received a short time ago information from many sources that the groups opposing the government are doing special efforts to kill us on the ground that we are the only bridge to Zionism and imperialism and moreover that we are giving Zionist education which is according to them racist education. And in order to cut off these ties and to break this bridge, the way they found is to kill us is to murder us. Considering this explanation, we are asking you to do anything in any way in your possibility to save our lives, without any doubt we will not be in life very soon and the action anyway will come to stand still when our life will be over. And now the judgment for life and for death for us is under your hands.

It was signed by five teachers, and the number of their families was listed alongside their names: 6, 3, 9, 8, 10. The last letter came in August, 1978:

I cannot find words which can express or stress the terrible situation of all the Jews here. Just to say that they all about to die, they don't know how to get out of the situation. Maybe they had in mind, and they hoped in their heart, that in such a situation, the Jewish people and the Jewish nation in general, would come to help, and they are waiting for this to happen every day because the urgent situation puts them in a terrible desperation. Without any alternative, they are just being transformed to slaves by their neighbors, and all the refugees who have left their places, who have been displaced, and who are without food and clothes, and just who would do anything to survive . . . And this thing is very much sorry, that it occurs when the state of Israel is already existing . . .

For some supporters of the tribe, appeals like these became impossible to ignore. They felt that a cry must go out, that people cannot allow themselves to become inured, indifferent to the survival of their fellow human beings. And for some Jews, the Falasha question boiled down to a Talmudic injunction: To save one life is to save the whole world.

The Falasha supporters saw parallels with events in recent history. Thousands of Jewish lives might have been saved from the Nazi extermination machine if early warnings had been heeded, if the subtle game of politics had not held sway over the American Jewish leadership, which constantly acquiesced to President Roosevelt's wishes to sweep the first news of the Holocaust under the rug.

Perhaps it is misleading to draw comparisons between Africa and Europe, Germany or Russia and Ethiopia; yet there are some striking parallels between the pogroms directed against Jews by Europeans, Arabs and Africans alike. The pogroms of today are being directed against a once mighty Jewish tribe, whose history is no less important than the history of German Jewry. In recent years, historians, anthropologists, musicologists and other scholars have begun to reveal the incredible story of the Beta-Israel tribe. The rich mythology, religion and history of the Falashas have important implications for both African and Jewish studies. It also tells us something about a lost tribe.

2

Ethiopia

Judith Yalo

In 1868 a member of the Yalo family, Yacob Yalo, was one of two Falasha boys taken from his village in Ethiopia to Palestine for instruction in Hebrew and modern Judaism. The man who brought them out of Africa, Professor Joseph Halevy, was a renowned Sorbonne Orientalist who had been sent by a French-Jewish organization to investigate stories of a tribe of Jews in the highlands of northwest Ethiopia, the ancient land known as Cush in the Bible. The most recent of those reports had been the sensational claims made by English Protestant missionaries who had been trying to convert the black African Jews since the 1840s. There had been many other reports during previous centuries—by explorers, merchants, travelers, soldiers—about the Jews of Ethiopia. But Halevy's journey marked the first real stirring of Jewish interest in the Falashas.

Halevy had traveled from his archeological dig in Yemen and entered Ethiopia from the south, arriving in Qwara, near Gondar, which was then the place of the orthodox Falashas, including many of the holy men. "Oh my brethren," Halevy said, "I am like you, an Israelite . . . a white Falasha." The Falashas trusted him and sent two of their brightest youths with him when he left Ethiopia.

Yacob Yalo eventually returned to Qwara—after fifteen years of education in Palestine and Europe—to teach his people about modern Judaism. But the Falashas, including Yalo's own family, resisted change in their religious practices. They continued to follow the laws of the Torah, the first five books of the Bible, and they wouldn't yet accept the Talmud, the rabbinical tradition of Judaism that was introduced long after the Israelite tribe that may be related to the Falashas had been exiled from the northern Kingdom of Israel. On Passover, the Falashas' high priest continued to follow the prescribed law in Exodus and sacrificed the lamb at sunset on an altar in the synagogue courtyard, sprinkling the animal's blood around the entrance to the building. But the Beta-Israel did share other Passover rites with Jews outside Ethiopia. They ate unleavened bread, called *kita*, during the seven days of Passover, the Freedom Festival; and the priest related the story of how Elohim had freed the Jewish people from bondage in Africa and resettled them in Israel. Passover remains the most meaningful of all festivals for the Falashas, who feel that they are still slaves awaiting the divine intervention that will take them to the land of Israel.

In 1941, during the Italian occupation of Ethiopia,

most members of the Yalo clan moved from Qwara to Begembdar Province, and one branch of the family built its homes in the village of Winega, about a day's walk from Gondar, the old imperial capital of Ethiopia. On the way, they had spent some time in Christian villages, among the Amhara who were their masters and the rulers of the hundreds of other tribes that make up Ethiopia. The Christians always said that the Falasha Jews "smell of water" because of their frequent ritual bathing. When the Yalos would leave a Christian village they would go to a stream to undergo purification rituals, having been "contaminated" by contact with idolators—which is how Christians are perceived. The Falashas would wash themselves and their clothes in the stream, and when they came to the first Falasha village, they would wait until sunset before entering.

This purification ritual has been abandoned by the Falashas in recent years.

The Yalo family's greatest treasure was a handful of books from the time of Halevy's visit. The books set them apart from other Falashas, especially after twenty-year-old Avraham Yalo learned to read them. He was already the father of a daughter and two young sons, and he wanted his children to be educated, and most of all, he wanted them to live in the newly independent state of Israel. They'd heard of the 1948 independence war from one of the Falashas in the town of Gondar. In Winega village, Rachel, Yalo's wife, gave birth to eight more children, three of whom died before the age of one. The family prospered and other close relatives came to live with them.

The males in the family did the farming, as elsewhere

in Ethiopia, while the women did the housework: drawing water, grinding corn or threshing *teff*—a grain that grows exclusively in Ethiopia—making honey mead, baking bread, gathering fuel, spinning cotton, tending a small vegetable patch and taking care of the children.

Yalo cultivated the soil with a primitive plow, fashioned by a Falasha blacksmith, mounted on a wooden frame and drawn by two oxen. Sowing began with the coming of the rainy season, and harvesting, using a sickle, began in September during the dry season.

As he plowed the fields owned by an absentee landlord, Yalo shouted and cracked his whip to keep the oxen moving along. Then he drove the animals around the threshing circle with their jaws bound together to prevent them from eating the grain. At night and during the rains, the family huddled inside the dark, round mud-wattle hut with its thatched conical roof—the Ethiopian *tekel*, which has no windows and only a single, low door. Yalo read to his children and explained the things he had struggled to learn about their religion and beliefs. He told them "Jewish stories" no different in spirit than the stories learned by Jewish children of the European ghetto or the Arab mellah. Yalo told them about the history of the tribe, how they were exiles in Ethiopia and strangers to the Ethiopians even after thousands of years.

His daughter Judith, a small, light-skinned girl bursting with energy and curiosity, especially liked to hear stories about the great Falasha queen, Yehudit, how she had vanquished the Amhara armies, destroyed Christian churches and conquered Axum a thousand years ago. But

Yehudit, the greatest heroine of the Beta-Israel tribe of Jews, is the devil incarnate to Christian school children, who are taught to hate her and who revile the Falashas. They call her Yehudit the Terrible and make a pun on her name, calling her "Yehudit Bud'it," meaning *buda*, the evil eye. The word is a curse and *buda* is used interchangeably with the word "Falasha," which means exile, stranger, and ultimately, devil.

"We were the greatest warriors in Africa," Yalo told his children. "For centuries, we lived in our own king-dom—until the *goyim* finally overcame us with the guns that the Portuguese gave them." The children learned the Biblical prayers, as well as Falasha stories like *The Death of Moses.* They said "Next year in Jerusalem" every year, not really knowing that it actually would come true for most of the Yalo family.

In 1960, when Judith was seven-years old, Yalo's children had their first tangible evidence of Israel in the form of a map brought by Azariah Gette, a Falasha linguist and educator who represented his tribe in Addis Ababa. Azariah came to the village to hire Yalo to teach at Uzava, where an Israeli group had built a school for the Falashas. He spread the map in front of the children and showed them where Jerusalem was located: Ethiopia was far away from everywhere, but not so far from Israel. Thereafter, the dream of Israel became an obsession with the Yalo children.

Avraham Yalo was glad to go to Uzava, where he had relatives. And the pay he would get for teaching, $12 a month, was a godsend. In Uzava village, as in Winega, the Amhara lord who owned the land that the Falashas worked as sharecroppers would come in person to the village once a year. His aides gathered tribute all year round—up to seventy-five percent of the serf's crop. The armed men of his entourage were contemptuous of all Ethiopians who were less Semitic looking than the Amhara and Tigre peoples, and they called the blacker Ethiopians *shangalla*, slaves. Judith wondered about it. For within her own family, and the tribe as a whole, there was a wide variety of features. She was light, with a thin Semitic nose and lips, while a brother and several of her cousins were ebony black, with negroid features.

Avraham Yalo told his children how the mixing of the tribes had begun thousands of years ago and how, because of slavery, it was still going on. Even the most enslaved of the tribes, like the Falashas themselves, owned slaves. Judith's grandparents had bought two girl slaves from the Oromo— the tribe whose slave name was Galla. All "big men" bought house slaves then. Her grandfather brought them from Shoa Province, from Addis Ababa, to the Yalo home in the northwest. And the two slaves had many children, but they never acquired husbands because the young Falasha men did not want them. The slaves' children remained servants in the next generation.

In keeping slaves, the Falashas were typically Ethiopian. But there was a difference: "They make proselytes of their slaves, and they treat them like members of the family," Protestant missionary J. M. Flad wrote in 1869. "They are not sold again and receive much better treatment than among the mahommedians." It was in keeping with the Torah (called *orit* by the Beta-Israel): among the Jews, treatment of slaves was not cruel.

Yalo had been living in Uzava for four years when the school where he taught was burned down by neighboring Christians who resented any attention the Falashas received from outside aid groups. So he moved his family to the rambling town of Gondar, where he paid rent on a corner of land and built his house. The Christians tried to stop him from moving in, and there was much trouble. For Yalo had built his house just outside the traditional boundary of the Jewish ghetto in Gondar—on Christian territory. But after a few years of intimidation, the family's presence was finally tolerated.

Yalo became a kosher butcher, buying many cows from the Christians, slaughtering them according to the laws of *kashrut*, and selling the meat to fellow Falashas. There was also a Moslem ghetto in Gondar, and Judith and her brothers and sisters felt much easier around these fellow outcasts. The Christian children constantly threw stones at the Falashas and taunted them about the "evil Jewish queen" who had tried to destroy Ethiopian Christianity.

There were many missionaries around Gondar, including a number of converted Falashas. A relative of Yalo's from the Woggera region had become a Christian. Although he was ostracized by his people, he kept trying to get other members of the family to go to the missionaries, promising them that their lives would be much easier if they renounced their Judaic faith. When Judith was twelve a "Jews for Jesus" type of group came through Gondar. Its members said they were Jews who accepted "all the Jewish holy books and Elohim, but also Jesus." The apostates were idolators in the eyes of the Beta-Israel, whether they were white Jews or black Jews. Judith thought the traveling missionaries were terrible people, all sweet smiles and holy deception, they frightened the Falashas. There was constant economic pressure from the Protestant missionaries, who monopolized medical services and schools in the area. But the efforts by the Christians only reinforced the Yalo family's determination to go to Israel. *Most* Ethiopians want to get out of their poverty-stricken country, but the Falashas were the only tribe with a place to go—Israel, home of their "ancestors"—for they believe that they are the children of Moses. Horror stalks everyday life in Ethiopia; and for Judith, growing up was a typically terrifying experience. In the Christians' market in Gondar, there were public hangings of criminals every sabbath—anywhere from one to fifteen persons were strung up for the public to watch.

It became obvious that unless one had a lot of money and could hire protection, living in Ethiopia meant to live in fear. Terror prevailed in town and countryside. In the villages, the *shiftas* would come from the forest. They would enter the houses in the village, eat their fill, take clothes, money, rifles, gold. If they weren't received well the host would be cut down in front of his wife and children. Police or army were never informed. They couldn't wipe out the bandit gangs, and the *shiftas* would take revenge—if one of their victims talked, everyone in the village would be killed or mutilated and the houses destroyed.

Avraham Yalo vowed to liberate his children from this peasant nightmare. He saved money for the day when they'd need it. And the first of his children was freed when Judith's older sister, Ruth, was six-years old and the opportunity came to send her to Israel with a youth group sponsored by the Jewish Agency. Ruth was sent to Kibbutz Kfar Batya along with eleven other Falashas. Most of them spent ten years in Israel and then were sent back to teach Hebrew in Falasha schools.

Ruth stayed on the kibbutz for eleven years, leaving after high school for nursing studies at a hospital near Tel Aviv. As soon as she had saved some money, she set out for Ethiopia to visit her family for the first time in fourteen years. Ruth and a friend flew from Israel to Kenya, but their flight onward to Addis Ababa was diverted to Sudan because of bad weather, and when the Sudanese saw that the women had Israeli passports, they arrested them. But they had luck—a rich Ethiopian living in Khartoum, a lapsed Falasha, heard about them and bribed the necessary officials to obtain their release.

Judith and her family in Gondar had been waiting apprehensively. Her mother thought Ruth might have been injured or killed—all they knew was that she'd been arrested by the Moslems. There was a party planned for her, and it was postponed and postponed again. Judith would ask about her sister every day after school. Finally, the Yalos heard that she'd arrived safely in Addis Ababa. The next day, when she arrived from the Gondar airstrip in a taxi, everyone was waiting for her, including a Christian family that had befriended the Yalos. Ruth dazzled them all: A high-cheek-boned, beautiful woman fashionably dressed. She brought three suitcases full of gifts for her family. Ruth's mother couldn't believe her eyes. She cried and then fainted.

Ruth stayed with them for three months before return-

ing to Tel Aviv. She thrilled her family and the other
Falashas of Gondar with stories about her life in Israel, and
she promised to send enough money for them to come one
by one. Two years later, in 1969, Yalo's son Yossi would be
the next to go. By then, it was getting more and more
difficult to leave Ethiopia—Haile Selassie's repressive regime did not encourage Ethiopians to visit other countries.
But Yossi went to the port of Massawa in Eritrea and got a
job as deckhand on a Red Sea freighter. Three days later he
jumped ship in Eilat, Israel's Red Sea port.

   He took any job he could get, and, like Ruth, saved
and sent money home. Judith's turn came three years later.
She was seventeen and she was determined to get an education, to leave Ethiopia and live in Israel. She left Gondar
with five other Falashas—two cousins and three of her
friends—heading for Asmara in Eritrea to get passports.
Judith had told her teachers in Gondar that she had to go to
a special hospital in Asmara for treatment—and so she
obtained a travel document that allows movement from one
province to another. The six Falashas arrived in Asmara in
twosomes, and Judith went to see an Interior Ministry official who knew her older brother. He tried to smooth the way
for her—getting a passport and a visa was always difficult
for the Falashas; only a few got through it all.

   Judith had written "Jewess" on some of her papers, and
this was a mistake—a Moslem clerk obstructed her because
she was trying to visit Israel. After two days of waiting and
pleading, one of the higher officials, who was from the
Gondar area, took care of her case. He helped the group
with some of the initial hurdles, but it wasn't enough.

Judith lied about her age—seventeen was underage—and she told police interrogators in Asmara that she was twenty-three. "What? You're still a little girl, who are you fooling?" they said to her. But Judith, feisty and tenacious, kept insisting that she was twenty-three.

The Falashas also got some help from an Israeli living in Asmara, but it still wasn't enough to get an exit permit. They had spent six weeks in Asmara trying to get visas when they were told that they could go back to Gondar and wait for news. From the post office in the town, Judith telephoned persons in Addis and Asmara who might be able to help, including a relative in the government. He could have done something, but was afraid to. After a month, she went to Addis Ababa to confront this relative and to demand his assistance. He told her, "You won't get out, it's too difficult and I can't help you—I don't want to get involved." One of her cousins went with Judith to see another "big man," but he also said that he was afraid to help. Haile Selassie's Israeli-trained secret police were everywhere. And the emperor, like so many of his predecessors, was determined to convert the Falashas to Christianity. He had vowed never to let them get out. The six Falashas submitted more and more documents—they had spent four months now trying to get travel papers. They pleaded that they only wanted to visit their brothers and sisters in Israel. Their hopes were constantly raised and then dashed. The officials in Asmara wrote to say, "All right, you'll get your visas in a few more days." But two days before Judith was due to get her documents, the government clerk wrote to say, "No, it's impossible."

They persevered finally, overcoming the maze of third world bureaucracy, and exit visas arrived at the Gondar post office.

Judith still had to go to the Israeli Embassy in Addis Ababa to present a letter from an Israeli taking responsibility for her and seeing to it that she didn't violate her tourist visa. She gave them a letter from Ruth. The embassy staff was cold and tried to discourage her from going to Israel, even for a visit. Judith didn't know that the Israeli Foreign Ministry had instructed the embassy to turn away Falashas trying to get to Israel. Christian Ethiopians, on the other hand, never had trouble getting tourist visas to visit Israel. Judith bought a boat ticket in Massawa, and like Yossi, went up the Red Sea to Eilat, the port near Etzion-Geber that had thrived in the days of King Shimshon and the Queen of Sheba, when Israel and Ethiopia were trading partners . . .

Shimshon Abebe

SHIMSHON POINTED to the thatched mud-wattle hut perched like a bird's nest among the trees above a green field of *teff*. "That's a Jewish home," he said. Shimshon Abebe and his friend Maro, another Falasha boy from the Begembdar area, were leading me through the beautiful rolling hills around their village, about one hundred and fifty miles north of copper-tinted Lake Tana, the headwaters of the Nile. Shimshon had spent the night in a roadside village, where I had sent him to rent a horse for me. He came back with a flea-ridden, sway-backed animal that cost fifteen cents a day.

It was early January, 1976, and I was staying in the area for a few days, gathering material for an article on the lost tribe of Dan. Thirteen-year-old Shimshon had attached himself to me at the first opportunity. Just as I was about to go to sleep on my first night on the village guest bed that was set up in the schoolhouse, there was a knock on the door: six young boys were standing shyly in the quiet, freezing cold night, all of them wearing brown sackcloth robes. They covered their mouths when they spoke, in the Ethiopian manner, pulling the material across their mouths and talking through it like masked surgeons. Shimshon Abebe, a very black youth made homely by bad teeth, introduced himself and one of his school friends. The two had just walked sixty miles from Azozzo, near Gondar, where they were attending a school that offered grades seven and eight—no Falasha schools went beyond the sixth grade. They had come for a two-week holiday—it was January, Christmas in Ethiopia, and Jewish children also got a vacation from school.

As he stood in the doorway, Shimshon said he had heard that twenty-five Falashas from his village and neighboring ones had been arrested while attempting to escape across the Kenyan border, far away to the south, and all were in prison. "Why doesn't the government of Jerusalem come to their rescue—to fight against Ethiopia?" he asked me in halting English. "Why don't the Jews of the world help us?"

Later, I learned that Shimshon was from a very poor

family. When he was ten, his father had to tell him that they didn't have enough money—$2.50 a year—to pay his school fees, and that he would have to give up his education. A British teacher in Gondar who traveled to outlying villages to teach English had taken an interest in Shimshon, one of his brightest students. The teacher gave him the five Ethiopian *birr* he needed for the school fees. Shimshon had never seen so much money so he couldn't be blamed for lavishing it on other things.

He was scolded severely afterward, but he got more money from the teacher and was able to continue his schooling. Shimshon set about acquiring an education with the goal of getting to Israel and eventually bringing his family: He was one of those who knew that things were looking bleak for his tribe . . .

Mulu Dese, the bespectacled assistant principal of the grammar school where I was staying, had asked me to sign the visitors' book soon after I arrived in the village. When Shimshon and his friends left, I took the ledger off the shelf near my cot and looked through it. Since the revolution two years earlier, a number of other visitors had come to the village, including an Israeli doctor who checked the people for parasites and other diseases. Before 1974 there had been a visit by an American study group, Moshe Dayan's first wife, Ruth; an Israeli ex-minister of transport; and Jewish couples from England and the United States.

There were other books on the schoolroom shelves: worn texts in Amharic and English, some Hebrew books for children, an old copy of Wolf Leslau's collection of the Beta-Israel's rich liturgy. There was also a Jewish Bible, and a leather-bound New Testament embossed with a gold cross—the headmaster was a Christian. The school had always been administered by Ethiopian Christians—under Haile Selassie and after him—and the current principal, an Education Ministry appointee, was a Tigrean, determined to bring Christianity to the Ethiopian Jews. The Falashas had no voice in how their schools were run.

Mulu Dese, who was also head of the staff of four Falasha and two Christian teachers, had a constant struggle with his Christian administrator over the teaching of Hebrew, which the Falasha teachers had learned in Israel.

In 1956 Mulu Dese, ten-years old, had been brought to Israel with other Falasha youths, and they lived, studied and worked at Kibbutz Kfar Batya. After four years, Mulu continued his education at a commercial school in Haifa for five more years. And after a decade in Israel, he came back to teach Hebrew and to help advance his people in Ethiopia. In his village, Mulu Dese was highly respected for his know-ledge. But the village had no real leaders because the Falashas have been more loyal to family than to community. It was difficult to change this, even though the necessity for strong leadership was becoming increasingly evident. Dese and the other teachers who had lived in Israel were constantly asked about the country that all of them missed so much. Among themselves, they reminisced constantly about Israel.

On my second day in the village I ate lunch in the home of Mulu Dese and his wife, Esther. They had three small children with another on the way. Esther, with her three-year-old daughter trying to help, served the staple

meal—*injerra*, a spongy pancake-bread made of *teff* grain
and topped with a sauce called *wot*. While we ate, Dese
turned on the radio to hear the news. He had the only
transistor in the village, and on rare occasions he could even
hear Kol Israel, the Israeli radio. During the Yom Kippur
War all of the villagers would come to the teacher's *tekel* to
hear BBC and Voice of America reports of the fighting.
Possession of this radio, and the fact that he had lived in
Israel, may have made Mulu Dese suspect in the eyes of the
Christians overseeing the Falashas' schools. In fact, he was
already a condemned man. Two years after my visit, he
would be imprisoned with the other teachers for being
"Zionist agents." Mulu Dese knew for years what fate was
waiting for him and for his people. He had lost all faith in
Israeli officials and in the Jews of the world. "They don't
hear our warnings. Perhaps they just don't want to."

IN THE AFTERNOON Shimshon took me to the hut of a
woman known for her ability to "interpret" dreams. This
unraveler of dream mysteries, a woman of about forty, put
aside the stick and spindle she used to spin raw wool and
welcomed us into her cool dark *tekel*. She related a dream
that several villagers had shared and offered her solution—
one that sounded either contrived or inspired: "If you dream
of water . . . the sea is on the land. When the water meets
the soil, it changes color. And someone passes over this
river . . . If the water turns red, the dreamer will leave his
land and get to Israel. But if the water is clear, or if it turns
brown, like Ethiopia, this means the man won't leave."

Passover is the most important Falasha festival because the Beta-Israel consider themselves to be slaves in Ethiopian bondage. This dream of Exodus—liberation—seems to be generated from the core of their beliefs. The woman told of a similar dream she had interpreted. A villager came to her and said: "I dreamed of *orev*"—Noah's raven, the scavenger bird prized for its ability to find dry land. "The *orev* came to our village. And I was traveling on this bird," the dreamer said. The woman's solution: "It means you will fly to Israel."

In recent years, these dreams of wishing for immigration to Israel have become stronger and more frequent, set off perhaps by promises and encouragement from Israeli and Western Jewish visitors. The dream has been fed by the apocalyptic visions of northwestern Ethiopia, the chaos of war and revolution that engulf the Falashas. There has been nothing like it among the Beta-Israel since the disastrous long march of the Falashas in the 19th century, when the tribe attempted to walk en masse to the Land of Israel. The Falasha false messiah who had convinced his people that the Red Sea would once again part for the Jews died before they reached the Eritrean coast, and thousands of other Falashas perished along the way.

ON A NARROW footpath winding between the conical huts, we met Kes Tefera and two other men who waited to show me the synagogue. Tefera, one of the area's six *cohenim*, wore a white turban, like all Christian and Jewish priests who follow the injunction in Exodus—"the sons of Aaron the priest shall wear tunics." The Levite priesthood usually follows family lines, as it was prescribed to Moses: There shall be an "everlasting priesthood, throughout their generations." The *cohenim* of Ethiopia, like those in Israel and other countries, claim direct descent from Aaron, brother of Moses. The Beta-Israel priest performs circumcisions, marriages and burials, and he conducts services, often accompanied by a light beat on a drum and cymbals, bells and gongs, at the end of which the Beta-Israel perform a haunting, Hasidic-like dance.

Kes Tefera showed me around the one-room mud and stone synagogue, which contained a Torah written in Ge'ez, Ethiopia's Semitic liturgical tongue. The structure was built so that the worshippers face toward Jerusalem when they pray before the Torah. There were few furnishings or other objects in the building: a couple of wooden benches and some Hebrew books donated by Jewish charities. The Israeli-trained teachers spurn the services, which still do not reflect modern Jewish laws and customs. There was a profound generation gap among many Falashas, and perhaps it is significant that Kes Tefera's son, who lives in Israel, became the Falashas' first ordained rabbi.

The religion the tribe follows is based mainly on the five books of Moses, the Pentateuch. It includes dietary and cleanliness laws; birth, marriage and death rituals; prayer; festivals, and, most importantly, observance of the sabbath. Falasha literature is heavily influenced by Coptic Christianity, but the tribe has some original works, such as *Commandments of the Sabbath*, in which the seventh day is portrayed as a female figure who personifies the heavenly world. All of the liturgy is in Ge'ez—but most Falashas are ignorant of their literature, and even the most learned priests, like Kes Tefera, have only a superficial knowledge of Ge'ez.

Kes Tefera was not interested in talking about religion just then—two of his sons were facing death, and the priest asked me what I knew about the incident that Solomon had asked me about when I first arrived. Twenty-five Falashas from surrounding villages had attempted to flee Ethiopia by crossing the Kenyan border, hundreds of miles to the south. It was an ill-conceived plan, devised by an Israeli supporter of the Falashas who had assumed a paternalistic role with the people he wanted to save. The plan was sanctioned by Jewish Agency officials whose interest in saving the Falashas was minimal. All twenty-five Falashas were arrested, including Kes Tefera's two sons—and there was a strong possibility that they would be executed within days.

This was the second time the pilot project for an "underground railroad" to Kenya had failed. A few weeks earlier, a group of four Falashas had made a trial run. They were met by two French Jews who had been hired on a per-head basis—the Jewish Agency would give them $500 for each Falasha that they got out. The two men apparently didn't worry whether some Falashas might be killed.

When their Land-Rover was stopped by Kenyan police they immediately gave up their passengers, who were taken back to the Ethiopians.

But even though the trial run had failed, the scheme was tried again, using the same two Frenchmen and an inexperienced Israeli Falasha. This time, instead of just four persons, the escape of twenty-five Beta-Israel villagers was attempted—people who had no sophistication whatsoever. One Israeli familiar with the operation was furious: "This wasn't like *aliyah beth*," he told me, referring to the illegal immigration to Palestine after World War II: "*Those* refugees had survived the concentration camps and they knew how to manage, to read and write. If you told them to show up in Rome on such and such a day, you knew they could do it. But the Falashas are naive, illiterate people from backward, upcountry villages—you can't expect them to fend for themselves."

The truck carrying the twenty-five Falashas had stopped *directly* in front of an Ethiopian police post at the border. It didn't take long to determine that these mountain tribesmen from the north were trying to get out of Ethiopia. They were slapped into prison. And the village where most of them came from was getting ready to go into mourning.

ON THE WAY back to the schoolhouse, which sits on top of a rise in the center of the village, we stopped at Kes Tefera's home—a compound of two *tekels* and a tiny hut, where the women stayed during menstruation. The priest's wife, a graying, emaciated African matriarch, burst into tears as she asked me about the fate of her sons, who were among those arrested. She was sure that they would be killed. I told her I couldn't help—and felt at a loss. I was invited inside the hut where the family lived amid huge grain bins made of sun-baked mud. A few goat and monkey skins, placed on the earth bench that curved out from the wall, served as the seat of honor. The faint light filtering through the low door highlighted the dust that seemed permanently suspended in air—dust that rises from the jars of grain and from chickens running in and out on the earth floor. The woman continued to cry and shake her head while one of her grandsons clutched shyly at her skirt. The toddler's eyes were caked with green-black flies that fed on an infection—millions of Ethiopians suffer from similar eye diseases.

Kes Tefera explained to his wife that I was just another Jewish tourist, powerless to do anything about their situation. She nodded sadly and asked me only to relate greetings to one of their other sons who had been in Israel for seven years and who had become the first Beta-Israel rabbi in history. The priest and his wife gave me a parting gift—a huge citron, like the *etrog* of the Succot holiday—and wished me a safe journey back to Israel.

SHIMSHON AND his friend led me back toward the main road, where bands of baboons romped through chickpea patches on both sides of the winding mountain path. The two boys greeted fellow Falashas and *goyim* as they passed by—*goy* is one of the few Hebrew words in the vocabulary of the Beta-Israel, who speak Amharic and Tigrean. Although their religion creates an enormous gulf between them and their Christian neighbors, physically, they look the same.

They live in strikingly beautiful country—hay colors mixed with shades of green and brown, deep-blue skies and the fascinating stale, grainy smells of Africa. Shimshon pointed to a far-off hill on the left—"missionaries," he said scornfully: very polite, devoted English Protestants intent on weaning these Jewish tribesmen from their incongruous beliefs, giving them crosses to wear alongside their medicine bags. For a century the missionaries had plotted to win the Falashas' souls for the Ethiopian Christian Church—up until most missionaries were expelled by the Marxists in 1977. The Falashas were a side-show battle in the Christian-Moslem struggle in Africa; but the missionaries had labored hard to convert this tiny yet significant tribe of Jews in the heart of Africa's first and greatest empire.

"Don't forget us," Shimshon said to me at the roadside village of Teda as I got on the bus for Gondar. It is what the Falashas have said to every Jew who has visited them.

Rafi Tarfon

HIS SHIRT was drenched in sweat from the intense heat: The January sun hit Rafi full blast as he walked with six other passengers from the battered DC-3 that bumped to its usual scary landing through the dust of Gondar's airfield. Rafi Tarfon was returning to his hotel headquarters in the town to wrap up business—it was his last month of work with the Falashas. ORT, the organization he was working for, had fired him for "insubordination" a few months after the international aid organization had taken over the project from the tiny Falasha Welfare Association, which was made up of Falasha support committees in England, Israel and the United States. The Falashas had been receiving between $30,000 to $60,000 a year. ORT promised to do much more, under a $2 million nonsectarian aid program for the whole of Gondar province. Rafi had vehemently opposed ORT's grandiose new plan, which he felt would mean even less aid for the Falashas. His new bosses in Geneva, who knew little about Ethiopia, disregarded his opinion. At the first opportunity they got rid of him. He had left himself open for dismissal when he bought three old rifles for the defenseless Beta-Israel tribe, supposedly using nonsectarian funds that had been designated solely for building schools and for medical services.

Now, in 1977, the gray-haired Israeli's twelve-year-long affair with Ethiopia was coming to an end.

Tarfon, at sixty, was still lean and energetic despite a number of bouts with some of the devastating diseases endemic to the country. His former wife, Rebecca, who had left Rafi and Ethiopia five years before, had lost her vision to an Ethiopian eye disease. But the threat of schistosomiasis, worms that invade the body, elephantiasis, or amoebic dysentery never persuaded Rafi to leave Ethiopia. He loved the country. And he had a special relationship with the Falashas—he too felt that he was a Jewish exile in Africa, a refugee from an increasingly corrupt society.   He believed that deadly Ethiopia was what kept him alive; and the news that he would have to leave hit him hard.

The taxi driver who took Rafi into town from the airfield knew his face well—there were only a handful of Europeans living in the town: two Christian missionaries, a scholar doing research on Beta-Israel history, and Rafi, the man who worked with the Jews. All of the foreigners would be leaving Gondar within the next few weeks. Gondar and Tigre provinces would be barred to outsiders by the revolutionary military government for the next year. The driver asked if Rafi could give him money to go to school abroad, if he could get him out of Ethiopia—everyone asked Rafi the same thing. Up ahead, they could see the outskirts of the sprawling town. Perched on a volcanic ridge at seven thousand feet elevation, Gondar sits midway between Lake Tana—the source of the Blue Nile—and the raw massif of the Semien, with its jagged peaks rising to fifteen thousand feet and higher.

As they drove through the settlement of forty thousand, they passed the compound of castles in the center of town—the core of Gondar founded by Emperor Fasiledes, who used Falasha craftsmen to build this landmark of black Africa. A giant tree that Fasiledes planted three hundred years before spreads its leaves over the heart of the old capital: "Justice" was handed out underneath this tree, and guilty and innocent alike were hanged from it. The practice was still going on. Thieves, opponents of the regime and innocent people were hanged in front of the market crowds, or shot in prison.

Long, pot-holed streets fan out from Gondar's center, with many tributary dirt roads stemming from all directions. Houses are crowded together: mud, rectangular, pan- or thatched-roof dwellings with no windows and one door—there is a definite security problem in Ethiopia. Homes are dense with smoke and cooking smells. Transportation around the town and neighboring villages is mainly by mule, or the ragged, battered horse-and-buggy taxis that ply the main road—there are very few motor vehicles. The main street is lined with pastel-colored stucco structures that glare in the midday light. One of the buildings is the Foggera, a two-story hotel where Rafi Tarfon kept a room. The hotel is set in an idyllic green spot on a rise above the main street. Its rooms and bungalows can accommodate forty guests, but the last tourists to pass through Gondar—

some Germans on a tour of Ethiopia's Historic Route—had left months ago and now Rafi Tarfon was the Foggera's only customer. He paid the cabbie the fare, put his suitcase in his room, and walked back to main street to get a coffee and to pick up his Land-Rover from the town's garage.

In Gondar people don't swarm all over a stranger, as in Addis Ababa; beggars are more restrained: deformed men with elephantiasis or birth defects can be seen parked by the roadsides. In the mornings, the beggars herd together to make the rounds, getting food scraps from the shopkeepers along the main street.

Rafi, a familiar figure after eighteen months in Gondar, had become a keen observer of Ethiopian life. During his years in the country he had worked for various international agencies as an agricultural expert and administrator, until his appointment to head the Falasha aid program. He had worked in the lowlands, in the plantation country of the southern Awash Valley, and in the east. But his favorite part of Ethiopia was Falasha country, in the mountain provinces of northwest Ethiopia; and Gondar was his base of operations. The hills around Gondar are baked a golden brown during the dry season, dotted with a few meager patches of growth. But the tallest hill, from which you can see the whole of Gondar, remains green with pine trees. There is a small Beta-Israel village up there.

Gondar has been the main crossroads for the Falashas since it was founded. Several Falasha families, like the family of the kosher butcher, live in Gondar itself, which has always had a small Jewish quarter. Until thirty years ago there was a terrible stigma on any Falasha who left his village for the big town. But that changed, mainly because of educational demands: Beta-Israel high school students stay in Gondar, and there is a boarding school for them.

Two teachers, Tedessa and Ephraim, met Rafi soon after he got back to Gondar. The Israeli's intense energy and enthusiasm for work, combined with a dignified manner and a wry sense of humor, had won him the respect and affection of the Gondar-area Falashas. Tedessa was especially close to him. Tedessa, a quiet, diffident man of thirty, didn't expect to get to Israel in the near future—not until the Ethiopians were somehow persuaded to let all the Beta-Israel go. In the meantime, he taught in a primary school and acted as Rafi's interpreter on excursions to the outlying villages.

The other teacher, Ephraim, who favored sporty, Western-style clothes and spoke American-accented English—a legacy of the Peace Corps—was a very different type than Tedessa: a cunning twenty-three-year-old man who was determined to go to America, freely admitting that Israel and the Ethiopian Jews meant nothing to him. Other Falashas in the town had warned Rafi that Ephraim "probably never was a Jew," saying that he was a Tigrean Christian who must have lived among the Falashas of that province. There were several Ethiopians who posed as Falashas in order to get a share of the $50,000 or so in Jewish aid going to the tribe—Ephraim had been marked out as someone not to be trusted. Rafi waited until after Ephraim left before he asked Tedessa about developments since his departure for Israel and Geneva three weeks before.

After lunch in the seedy dining room of the nearby Makonnen Hotel—Rafi twice had been felled by Makonnen

food poisoning—he and Tedessa met with a delegation of
Falasha women teachers. Rafi promised to visit their remote
village and inspect a school that needed repair. He made
arrangements for the trip later in the week—he could go
only so far with his Land-Rover, then he would have to trek
by foot for a day to reach their settlement. Many men half
his age would have difficulty making such a strenuous trip.
But Rafi kept in top shape, and his stamina and agility
surprised the Ethiopians. Even though he had only a month
left on the job, he worked as hard as usual. Rafi was stirred
deeply by the desperate situation of the Beta-Israel. But he
was also suspicious of some supporters of Falasha immigration to Israel, people who he felt knew next to nothing
about Ethiopia or the Beta-Israel tribe, bleeding hearts from
Israel or America who might be adding to the Falashas'
troubles.

Rafi thought that the Falashas who were already living
in Israel were another case entirely, a world apart, no longer
"Falashas." Personality and group conflicts among the three
hundred Beta-Israel in Israel were reflected in Ethiopia, and
he had only recently arranged a truce between the squab-
bling Tigre Falashas and their kinsmen in Begembdar Province, now renamed Gondar Province.

Tarfon's day-to-day activities were out in the open,
unlike that of his predecessor, an inexperienced English Jew
who had worked in a semi-secret manner until he was
arrested and expelled by the Ethiopians. The authorities had
recognized Rafi Tarfon as the Jewish representative, aiding
the Falashas in education and health. The revolutionary
regime had even offered Rafi some help—Pioneer Youth

members to aid in the fight against ninety-seven percent illiteracy. The national and local police were also aware of Tarfon's activities and approved of them. But this carefully constructed relationship would be changed by the ORT experts, who dismissed Tarfon a few months after they took over the program, submerging it in a big nonsectarian aid project for the whole province.

Delegations of Falashas came to Gondar from far across the mountains to see Rafi Tarfon. One strong old man, accompanied by two young Falashas, hiked for eight days before reaching a major road leading to Gondar. The man asked Rafi about getting money to build a school in remote Woggera, where there are about one thousand Beta-Israel. Some of them live in areas so steep that even a mule can't transport goods to them.

The tribal elder, garbed in an immaculate white *shamma,* the Ethiopian toga, was a fabled survivor among his people. During the Italian occupation of Ethiopia, Woggera natives kept up a guerrilla war against the invaders. The Italians, plotting revenge, lured thirty-three Falasha villagers and thirty other Ethiopians into a trap, saying only that "the government wants to see you." They were herded together and shot—except for this one survivor, who had recovered consciousness hours after the massacre and crawled away from the heap of bodies.

After a short siesta in the afternoon, Rafi drove to a school building on Gondar's outskirts, where he was going to meet with prospective teachers for first and second grades in the village schools. Fourteen Falashas were waiting for him, all teenagers. Rafi spoke to them through his interpreter—only two of them knew any English, and they had learned only a few words of Hebrew. They had all taken tests and were waiting for the results, which Rafi promised to deliver in a few days. If hired, they would be sent to the smaller villages and be paid $39 a month—a very high salary in Ethiopia. One of the budding teachers, Alibal, a buck-toothed, stuttering boy of sixteen, dominated the question period. "When can I get a scholarship?" he asked, a question that really meant: When am I going to be sent to Israel? Rafi replied that after a couple years of teaching the boy might qualify for further training and aid, but that it was a bit premature for him to try to get a scholarship before his job had even begun. "The idea is to serve the community, to help the village children," Rafi said, aware that his plea fell on deaf ears.

Alibal also questioned Rafi about servants for the teachers—who would cook their food? For cooking is anything but an instant affair in the villages. Alibal also wanted to get "medicine," meaning birth-control pills, so his woman cook would not get pregnant. He would be able to have intercourse with her, not marry her, and still have good food. Otherwise, either she would have his children and he'd be forced to marry her, or he wouldn't be able to have sexual relations with her—and then the food would be bad "because she wouldn't care just for the money." After his long discourse and many giggles, the teenager said, "I embarrassed." Tarfon's advice to him was to solve his own sexual problems. And he wondered how his successor would deal with these tenth-grade students who were becoming teachers.

Rafi Tarfon's first contact with the Beta-Israel occurred when he was the same age as the young students in front of him. It had begun forty-five years before, when he was a high school student in Germany. A Falasha youth, one of those brought to Europe by Professor Halevy's disciple, Jacques Faitlovitch, entered the Jewish school in Hamburg, in 1932, and he and Rafi became friends. Tarfon fled Nazi Germany in 1938, going to Palestine on Youth Aliya—the Palestinian Jewish organization that brought young people to the Jewish homeland. But he always kept in touch with his Falasha friend, who fought with the British during World War II and then returned to Ethiopia. The two men were still seeing each other regularly in Addis Ababa in 1977.

During the first years in Ethiopia, Rafi had felt that the Falashas were no different than other Ethiopians and that they had no solid claims to Jewishness. But after he came to know them he completely reversed his opinion, telling other Israelis, "They are as Jewish as you or me."

Rafi's former employer was Koor Industries, the conglomerate run by Israel's Labor Party federation. It had been his plan in 1975 to send seventy Falashas to Israel as workers for Koor; but the group had been stopped by the Ethiopians after the Israeli news media publicized that they were on their way. Rafi blamed an official of the Falasha support committee who had told reporters that the seventy were "coming this week," even though the plan was still in its formative stage. The announcement was broadcast by Israel Radio and was monitored in Addis Ababa by the Labor Ministry. The news was framed in a way that made it sound

critical of Ethiopia. Immediately afterward, Rafi was summoned—in a hospitable, Ethiopian manner—to explain
about these seventy people who he had selected for work in
Israel. "Are most of them or all of them Falashas?" they
asked him. Well, yes, he replied, claiming that whereas
black workers from abroad ordinarily would live separately
from whites in countries like England or France, the
Falashas would not have a "black problem" in Israel, where
they would blend beautifully into the country's polyglot
society: They were coreligionists who shared a "common
language," he said—in fact, few of the seventy knew any
Hebrew. His explanation was more or less accepted and the
matter was then dropped—but it spelled the end to Falasha
emigration for the next two years.

Rafi had taken on the job of "Jewish envoy to the
Falashas" because there was no one better qualified to do it.
He dreamed of an Ethiopian-Israel alliance, and he wanted
to see the Falashas armed in their struggle to survive attacks
by the various rebel forces that were threatening to wipe out
the tribe.

But the Israeli government under the Labor Party was
indifferent to the Ethiopian Jews, and this drove him to
despondency. He knew that Falashas were being killed in
several provinces, that the threat to their existence was very
real. During one leave in Jerusalem, he had made the rounds
of government officials, trying to persuade them to act. It
was just before the election in May, 1977—Labor was about
to be thrown out of power for the first time in twenty-nine
years. Friends told him that he was wasting his breath, that
the government wasn't doing anything for the destitute

Ethiopian Jews "because they're considered to be *schvartzes*." Rafi went back to Ethiopia, determined to do whatever he could for the Beta-Israel. When his ex-wife heard he was going back to Ethiopia, she bought him a burial plot.

THE FALASHAS appreciated how hard Rafi worked for them, his efficient military manner—he had been an officer in Israel's War of Independence—and the progress he was making to keep the schools going, build new ones, run the crude dispensaries, train paramedical workers and teachers. They didn't know yet that he was being pulled out. It was hard for him to tell them he would be leaving in a few days. Tarfon drove to Teda, a large mixed village in which Christians and Jews divided into two camps. Tarfon had been directing the building of a school; and he met once again with the village's four Falasha teachers and the *cohen*, or priest, who had two sons in Israel. The priest was very proud of his boys; the mud walls of his home were decorated with pages torn from *B'Mahane*, the Israeli Army magazine, which his sons had sent to him.

Rafi discussed the building of the new school, the cost of windows and wooden lintels—fifty Ethiopian *birr*, or $25, for a blackboard and seventy-five *birr* for the laborers. He and the teachers spoke in Hebrew, which was translated into Amharic for the priest. It would be hard for these people to comprehend Tarfon's shocking news, which he didn't tell them until they walked back toward his Land-Rover: "I've been fired by my boss in Europe," he said, "Someone else will be sent soon to help you complete this work."

Rafi thought ORT's ambitious $2 million plan would

eventually have tragic results. "ORT is a disaster," he told an Israeli friend in Nairobi, just before returning to Jerusalem in 1977. Although ORT officials gave credit to Rafi for his accomplishments during his eighteen months of service, they weren't interested in his advice. It broke his heart, for he thought that his firing spelled doom for the Falashas. He had reason to believe that—the signals were clear . . .

Azariah Gette

UNTIL THE revolution brought tourism to a standstill, Wallaca, a few minutes by horse-and-buggy from Gondar, was a minor tourist attraction for travelers in northwest Ethiopia: It was the "Jews' village," where hawkers sold small ceramic statuettes—Solomon and Sheba embracing in bed, a Lion of Judah with a Star of David on its head—and other items specially crafted for the visitors, who included a few Western Jews curious to see the primitive blacks identified as their brethren.

Before the Italian occupation in 1936, Wallaca village was an important center for Beta-Israel tribesmen coming from the Woggera region. It remained a crossroads for Falashas coming to Gondar from the west and north. It was the home of the Beta-Israel high priest, Aryeh Ben-David, until he was spirited away to Israel in 1977. And it was also the birthplace of Azariah Gette, who became the tribe's most prominent representative. The Beta-Israel have no official chiefs or leaders but Gette became a spokesman for

his people because of his education and reputation as a
leading scholar—not because of any special family background. His father had been a weaver in Wallaca, and
during the rainy season, like all the men of the village, he
ploughed a small patch of land belonging to a Christian
landowner.

Azariah's parents reared eleven children in their one-
room hut, scratching out an existence in one of the poorest
countries in the world. The family's feudal landlord demanded most of their crops: they would have been slaughtered had they missed a single payment.

In 1921 Professor Jacques Faitlovitch, the French Jew
who followed in the footsteps of his teacher at the Sorbonne,
Halevy, passed the rainy season in Wallaca; and Azariah was
among the village children who studied Hebrew with him
every night. By the end of the rains, every one of
Faitlovitch's students wanted to go to Palestine, the Land of
Israel. Most parents refused to send their children abroad—
the concept was too new and uncertain for them to consider.
But one of Faitlovitch's older students, Yermeyahu, a
relative of the Gettes, persuaded Azariah's parents to let him
go.

Azariah was eleven when he and three other Falashas
left Ethiopia. Two of them went to Palestine, one to Italy,
and one to Switzerland. After he had spent two-and-one-half
years in a *yeshiva* in Jerusalem, studying Hebrew and the
Talmud, Azariah went with Faitlovitch to Frankfurt, where
he learned German and Yiddish. Two years later, he
continued his education at a Jewish boarding school in
Baix-Lex-Bains, Switzerland, where he studied French and

Hebrew. Two of the other Falasha students in Europe died of tuberculosis; and the third, Avraham Baruch, was sent back to Addis after he, too, contracted TB.

Faitlovitch's first pupil had been Emmanuel Tamrat, who became a professor and director of the teacher training college in Addis Ababa until the Italian occupation in 1936, when he escaped to England. Tamrat would become one of the few Falashas allowed to go to Israel—he represented Ethiopia as counsel in Jerusalem until his death in 1968. Another Faitlovitch student, Tedessa Yacob, became Ethiopia's finance minister. But he was a great disappointment to his fellow Falashas. "He forgot that he was a Jew," Azariah said of him.

After Azariah completed his education in Switzerland, he returned to Addis to assist Professor Tamrat at the teacher college. When Tamrat escaped—he was on the fascists' wanted list—Azariah stayed in the capital to run the college. When the Italians closed the school, Gette went to work for some merchants—he had to make enough money to take care of sixty Beta-Israel students from the Gondar area who were living in Addis Ababa and who depended on Azariah to feed them.

Azariah wheeled and dealt in coffee for two years, until his name was added to the Italians' wanted list—the fascist police had intercepted an incriminating letter Azariah sent to Tamrat. Azariah fled to Oromo country in Wallaga, learned the language of that tribe and stayed for three years. There were gold mines there—some believe they are the same deposits mined in the Queen of Sheba's day—and Azariah became chief supervisor of two hundred miners.

When the Italians withdrew in 1942, he returned to Addis Ababa to head the department of schools. But when his office was expanded by the emperor to include supervision of mission-run schools, he quit: Azariah saw a report that the church mission to the Jews had baptized four thousand Falashas. He vowed that he wouldn't help the Christians destroy his people. For the next twenty-five years Azariah worked for various small Jewish aid groups, channeling the tiny contributions from world Jewry to the Falashas. Azariah Gette has said that his whole life was to help his people. But his critics, including some of the Falashas from Tigre, charged that he helped himself and his friends and did little for the main body of Ethiopian Jews. Azariah, gray-haired and dignified at age seventy, countered that he was being slandered, and that the internal tribal intrigue and rivalry—something endemic to Jews and Ethiopians alike—only served to delay action to bring his tribe to Israel.

ASA AZARIAH, Gette's eldest son, is a princely looking, guarded man, quiet but insistent, and there is a slow-burning anger in him for those who have blocked the rescue of his people. Asa knows he is different from most Falashas because of his urban background and college education in Israel. But he didn't set himself apart from other Ethiopian Jews; and he shares much in common with Falashas brought up in even the remotest villages.

From the age of four, his father had told him about the Jewish people. Azariah Gette had wanted to send all of his children to Israel in 1955, when the U.S. Women's Mizrahi

group provided funds to send a small number of Falasha
children to Kibbutz Kfar Batya. But Ora, the children's
mother, wouldn't agree. Azariah continued to teach his
children about Falasha traditions and history, and they grew
up with the stories of the Torah. Asa and his brothers and
sisters would pursue their father's life-long dream of going
to Israel.

When Asa was six and the family moved from the city,
north to Gondar, he discovered for the first time that his
people were still despised by their Christian neighbors, who
called them *buda* or *kayla*—possessors of the evil eye,
sorcerers who sucked the blood of young Amhara women
and babies. It was a big change for Asa. In Addis Ababa, no
one knew what a Falasha was, or what it meant when you
said you were a Jew. But they knew in Gondar. And it was
hard for the Gette family until they moved back to Addis
Ababa four years later.

There were only a handful of Falashas in the capital,
and for religious reasons—celebrating Jewish holidays and
keeping a kosher home—Asa's family lived a relatively
isolated life. But his friends were Christians, and he never
encountered any anti-Jewish prejudice.

Asa traveled with his father frequently, visiting remote
Falasha villages in the mountains. The people were suspicious of the city-dwellers because of the stigma applied to all
Falashas who leave the village, but Asa overcame the
hostility by spending more and more time in the backcountry. He developed a special interest in those of his
people who had become lapsed Jews. In previous centuries,
tens of thousands of Falashas were forced to choose between

conversion and death. A few of these converts became the Marranos of Ethiopia, secretly practicing Judaism in the steep mountain gorges outside their villages.

Asa had spent time with the tribe of fifteen hundred people in Addis Ababa called the Moreka, who he was convinced were among the lost Jews. Like the Falashas, who were Ethiopia's first metalworkers, the Moreka people also work with iron—which is the source of the evil eye blood libel that Christian Ethiopians apply to the Falashas. Asa was seventeen when he went with his father, two Falasha elders and a *cohen* to visit some of the Moreka in Addis Ababa, "to see if they were Jewish or not." They walked to the Moreka quarter on a sabbath day, and found that the Moreka observed almost the same religious traditions of the Beta-Israel.

Asa recognizes the strong connections between Judaism and Ethiopian Christianity, stemming from the Christian belief that the Ethiopians are the Second Zion. But the Falashas—and the Moreka—have far deeper ties with Judaism, Asa had found, and he disagreed vehemently with Ethiopia scholars like Edward Ullendorff who discount the Falashas' Judaism. Asa knew that if the gates of Israel were opened up and it was possible to leave Ethiopia, thousands of Ethiopian Christians would claim to be Jews. But the Falashas say that they know which families converted, going back several generations. And these Ethiopians, if they wished to disavow Christianity and return to their people, would be taken back into the community. Given the history of slavery and religion in Africa, it could mean hundreds of thousands of black Africans claiming they are Jews.

The Falashas always ran into formidable opposition whenever one of the few who could raise the money tried to go to Israel. Most of the one hundred and twenty Falashas who had managed to reach Israel before 1975, when they were recognized as Jews, had either jumped ship in Eilat or come disguised as Christian pilgrims, wearing big crosses around their necks. Even Asa and two of his brothers, Yosef and Yisrael, had run into serious problems at the Israeli Embassy in Addis Ababa, despite the fact that their father had powerful friends in Israel. A Christian who asked for a visa to visit Jesus' tomb would immediately get one, but if an Ethiopian Falasha asked for an Israeli visa he was actively discouraged, kept waiting for hours, humiliated. There was no more embassy after 1973, when Ethiopia joined with most of the rest of Africa in breaking diplomatic relations with Israel. That solved the minor nuisance of the Falashas for Israel's Labor Party government. With the revolution in 1974, it became harder than ever for a Falasha, or any other Ethiopian, to get out of the country.

AZARIAH GETTE'S youngest son, Yonatan, came the closest to death in getting to Israel. In 1977 he fled from murder squads in Addis Ababa to a remote Jewish village far from the nightmare capital. Addis Ababa is a horrifying city even in the best of times: The "new flower" of the plain swarms with badgering crowds, brown dust, smoke and flies in the frenetic marketplace. Strangers are descended upon by the hungry horde: clinging bootblacks and hustling hangers-on, a weird gallery of whores and grotesque beggars swathed in filthy burlap rags. And for many months during the terror of 1977 and 1978, crews of streetcleaners picked up the bullet-riddled bodies every morning, tossing them into battered trucks that pump clouds of black diesel exhaust into the air. On May Day weekend, about five thousand high school students were slaughtered.

Azariah Gette's youngest son was the only boy in his neighborhood to escape the executioners. Thousands were being murdered in the damp jails and dark streets, in courtyards near the dead Emperor's palace and in ditches outside the rambling marketplace. Yonatan had been arrested twice before the big roundup and massacre. He was in tenth grade at Menelik II High School at the time of his first arrest. It was during a nationwide labor strike shortly after the army revolution in 1974. Soldiers and policemen waving Uzi sub-machine guns swooped down on the school and arrested the entire student body. The authorities, some of them officious, mean-spirited Marxist-Leninists, questioned them in the classrooms. "Who made you strike?" they asked with cold authority. Every student was terrified, knees shuddering—the eyes of the inquisitors reflected an ideological fervor for murder-as-object-lesson. But it was still early then in the military's reign of tactical terror, and only a handful of children were to be punished—immersed in hot oil, sexually tortured or thrown out of windows from the fourth floor of the school building, left to die writhing in the dust of the road. Yonatan and the rest were held for three days in various frightening prisons and then released.

Yonatan was arrested again twelve months later as he walked with three friends in the garbage-strewn streets of the Piazza, the decayed, formerly European-run shopping quarter. Soldiers took the students' identity cards and giggled in a menacing way. They slapped them around a little and then handcuffed them. But in this atmosphere, where whim sometimes diverts the course of terror, the three were released after only perfunctory questioning.

Yonatan's third arrest was much more serious. Just before dawn, army jeeps and trucks came screeching into the street of "bourgeois" dwellings where Yonatan lived— homes belonging to government clerks and small traders. Soldiers shot open the doors and tore the houses apart. The rampage was all over by six o'clock that morning. Everyone who looked remotely like a student was rounded up, still sleepy-eyed after being rousted from bed. Every house on the block was searched, and twenty-one young people were taken away from their families. Similar scenes were taking place throughout the city.

Yonatan told the security police that he had only just returned to Addis Ababa from Gondar, where he had been teaching primary school, and that he had only come back to take his 12th grade exams. It was verified that Yonatan was a new teacher, no longer a student *per se*—a crucial distinction. For at that point in the revolution, the regime had decided to kill all of the students, not the teachers. They let Yonatan go.

Two days later, on Monday morning, thousands of parents got their children's clothes back, blackened and riddled with bullet holes. The government brought the bodies to the center of town, dumped them at Menelik hospital, and demanded that the parents pay $50 for each bullet hole before the corpse would be given to them. On Yonatan's street, a former navy captain lived with his wife and his six sons—all his children were murdered that day. Addis Ababa had been turned into a charnal house.

Yonatan walked many days north to the village where he would hide for four months. He received refuge from his people in the rugged highland massif, country dotted with purple and pink irises, baobab and mimosa trees, fields of soft-green *teff* and flocks of blue-gray birds—what the country's national airline once advertised as "Beautiful Ethiopia." It is a beauty caught in a land remarkable for horrible disease, devastating famines, massive swarms of locusts and the constant tension of violence. "Hunger, ignorance and disease bestowing their bounty all over the country," in the words of novelist Danachew Worku; "Ethiopia is God's way of putting an end to things."

In a pastoral village encircled by the towering Semien range where his ancestors had once maintained their independent kingdom, Yonatan had time to think about the fate of the Beta-Israel; how his tribe had become untouchables, objects of superstition and mockery, impoverished and backward mountain people. And in his own lifetime, he had learned firsthand that the prospect of annihilation of the Falashas had grown alarmingly. He felt that his people were at the end of their ancient history, but he experienced a religious vision: Israel would rescue its black sheep, just when their doom seemed certain.

3

Sons of Moses

The Sin of Ham

From beyond the rivers of Ethiopia my suppliants, even the daughter of my dispersed, shall bring mine offering.
(*Zephaniah 3:10*)

Scholars who are skeptical that the Beta-Israel are Jews point to the lack of solid fact to support the tribe's claim. But there are substantial sources—in folklore, religion, history, and anthropological studies—and they combine to make a convincing argument that the pariah Beta-Israel of Ethiopia are Jews. Their official recognition as Jews by the Israeli government in 1975 was based only in part on this evidence.

The following pages make an attempt to describe some of the tribe's links to other Jews, from Biblical traditions to the Beta-Israel's "magical" knowledge of metallurgy, Ethiopian queens and Jewish kings, the Temple's gold and the Ark of the Covenant, the centuries-long Ethiopian-Jewish war, and legends of the ten lost tribes. The story

57

stems from the geneology of Genesis and touches on
traditions of Moses, Solomon and Sheba, the Assyrian
conquest, the ancient Jewish garrison in black Africa,
Ethiopia's medieval crusades, Jewish travelers, false mes-
siahs, the advent of the missionaries, and finally, Israel's
rediscovery of the lost tribe of Dan—the Beta-Israel.

The leading Ethiopia scholar of this century, Conti-
Rossini, wrote that "Judaic nuclei" probably existed in
Ethiopia before the conversion of Axum to Christianity in
the fourth century. "The Falashas then would be descendants of those Ethiopians who, already Judaized, did not
convert to Christianity. Popular traditions in Ethiopia also
ascribe to such an explanation."

Many scholars have identified the Ethiopian tribe that
intermarried with Jews as a branch of the Agaw, the
aboriginal Ethiopians. The Agaw had resisted Christianity
from the time of its introduction; most of the tribe
worshipped idols, while other clans adopted Judaism, which
had penetrated Ethiopia for centuries and which was again
spreading rapidly in Ethiopia and Yemen between the
fourth and sixth centuries, when a Jewish king, Dhu-
Nuwas, ruled in neighboring South Arabia.

But Beta-Israel history before 1270 is based mostly on
speculation: There is no hard proof regarding the tribe's
origins.

Professor Robert Hess divides Beta-Israel history into
three stages: The first, prehistoric, period, deals with
speculations on their origins until the first direct references
to the Falashas, during the early 14th century reign of Amda
Seyon; the second, historic, stage is chronicled by Ethiopian

and European writers from the 14th century to the 17th century; the third stage, termed the "period of disintegration," spans the 17th century to recent times.

Jews are a subdivision of the human species, not a "race" in scientific terms—race describes only biological differences among people. There is no intention here of proposing that Africans are really Jews who went south during the Exodus—or that Jews are really Africans who went north.

Contention surrounds even the most dispassionate arguments about race, with advocates of rival disciplines predictably attacking each other. Politics and prejudice enter the picture. For certain populations, a fiercely defensive reaction is almost automatic—the Jews have more reason to be wary of race theorizing than most other people. Black Africans have also suffered horribly through the centuries in consequence of race theorists and their followers; and one must enter such territory in trepidation. But the question arises in any discussion about the Beta-Israel—can black Africans (or, for that matter, white Russians) be Jewish? The answer is: Of course. "Jew" is a religious and cultural phenomenon; it has nothing to do with race. Anthropologist Ashley Montagu has written: "It is generally agreed that all men belong to the same species, that all were probably derived from the same ancestral stock, and that all share a common patrimony."

American writer John A. Williams noted that the "genetic exchanges" that took place along the Africa-Middle East trail are "the kind of material people have never been able to deal with in a rational way. Their emotions leak out, and the weight of history in terms of what people think they are is crushing . . . Most of us subconsciously shy away from what may have been a common past. And it seems to me that Jews most represent that historic link . . . The Falashas are far older than 2,500 years; they have to be . . ."

Racial and tribal origins are an important element in the story of the black African Jews, figuring as well in the common background shared by two ancient lands, Israel and Ethiopia.

Connections between the Middle East and Africa have been proven not only by historical studies but also by geological and biological surveys, zoological research—the scientific study of man. Once, it was all joined together geographically: Ethiopia and Arabia, Egypt and Israel. Today, as nowhere else on earth, Ethiopia and Israel reflect an incredible diversity of language and tribe.

The word Abyssinia, *habasha* in Ethiopic and *habash* in Hebrew, connotes mixture of races. And more than seventy languages are spoken among Ethiopia's twenty-eight million people. It is a country that has been called "a museum of peoples," a characterization that is equally applicable to Israel. The Danakil and Oromo and Amhara are worlds apart within the Ethiopian empire; in another way, so are the Georgian Jews and the Moroccan Jews, Polish Jews and Indian Jews—a few of the seventy populations in the Israeli mosaic.

People mix. Within almost every tribe, there is a wide spectrum of skin colors and facial features—whether it is the tribe of Judah or the Agaw tribe. Most Ethiopia scholars have stated categorically that the Beta-Israel are a branch of

the Agaw, as are the Qwara and the so-called half-Jews, the
Hebraic-pagan Kemant. Wolf Leslau suggested that most
Falashas resemble the Amhara, but that many have the
physiognomy of the Bogos, another Agaw people living in
Eritrea. Altogether, scholars have identified eleven branches
of the Agaw family, numbering two hundred and fifty
thousand.[1] The Cushitic, or Negroid, Agaw were the
original inhabitants of Ethiopia, but they have long been
dominated by the Abyssinians, the Semitic Amhara and
Tigre tribes. These two people, who have intermixed with
the Agaw and the other tribes, probably came from South
Arabia. The Amhara and Tigre share some anthropometric
features with Semites,[2] but their very large eyes are a
distinct feature they do not share with other African or
Asian peoples.

The Agaw were gradually driven, in prehistoric times,
toward the south and west by incoming peoples—the
Yemenite Semites, according to several experts.

The Falashas themselves disdainfully reject the contention that they are Agaw tribesmen, expressing a contempt
many Africans have for darker Africans. They admit that
there has been a great amount of intermarriage, but they
prefer to be identified with the Amhara and Tigrean tribes
whose features are less negroid than that of the Agaw or
Oromo, for example. The tremendous range of physical
features among the Falashas belies this claim: some have

---

[1]Falasha, Kemant, Bogo, Damot, Wayto, Hamta, Bilen, Awiya, Kumfal, Hamir
and Qwara.

[2]The word "semitic" is the invention of an 18th century German linguist, who
derived it from Shem. Many scholars deplore the use of this term to mean a
race—the Semitic race, in their view, is a pseudo-scientific myth.

Arabian yellow-brown complexions and thin noses, others are coal black and thick-lipped negroid types.

Classification of Africans into "Hamites" and "Negroes" is based on a lot of guesswork about race and migration routes. A biological survey of Ethiopian tribes by Israel's Tel Hashomer Hospital in 1962 failed to show how much mixing occurred between the populations of Arabia and Ethiopia—it remains a mystery.

WHERE DID the division of people begin? Genesis traces the nations of the earth to the sons of Noah, and chronicles the Biblical progenitors of races and tribes: Ham and Japhet and Shem. They are of particular importance in discussing ancient Ethiopians and Israelites and the mix that came to be called Falashas. Ethiopia in the Bible was Cush, a major part of Punt—the entire Nile Valley south of Egypt, including Nubia. It lies along the most extensive rift on earth, which stretches from Syria to Mozambique. The Greeks translated the Hebrew name Cush as "Ethiopia" in the *Septuagent,* meaning "Land of the Burnt Faces." Punt is the ancient Egyptian name for "God's Land"—Ethiopia.

In Genesis, the sons of Ham were Mizraim (Egypt), Phut (Libya), Canaan (Palestine) and Cush (Ethiopia). Ham's children were cursed, the Bible says, because of their father's transgression—the Sin of Ham. Ham saw that his father Noah was drunk and naked in his tent, and he was insensitive to his father's honor. He informed his two brothers, Shem and Japhet, who immediately covered their father to save him from shame. When Noah sobered up, he put a curse on Ham and his progeny, the founders of four nations. Special wrath was directed against the founder of Palestine: "Cursed be Canaan, the lowest of slaves to his brothers."

Needless to say, the Biblical passage relating the etiology of races and countries has been attacked in modern times as a hate-inspiring exegesis. W. E. B. Dubois, the American black historian, put the word Hamitic—derived from Ham—in quotes, dismissing the whole notion of descent from a cursed ancestor.

The achievements of black Africa were always denigrated by white scholars until recent generations, and they constantly referred to influences and migrations of people from outside Africa, tribes who brought the light of civilization to the backward negro. But since the independence of most of Africa from colonial rule, this posture has been reversed.

Hamite and Semite still remain controversial words in a world of misnomers. In North Africa, two countries called Arab are inhabited mainly by Hamitic people—Morocco's Berbers and the Egyptian *fellah* are not Semites. But for the sake of convenience, the terms Hamite, Cushite and Semite continue to be used.

Among Ham's descendents were the Babylonians/ Sumerians,[3] a people who developed one of the earliest civilizations. Ham's grandson, Nimrod, built the Tower of Babel.

---

[3]The ancient Biblical association between Ham's descendants and Babylon might account for the Jewish tradition, discussed later, that Nebuchadnezzar was the son of Sheba's queen, who was also a Hamite.

Some scholars have said that Cush may not refer to Africa at all, but to a place in Mesopotamia, where Nimrod founded Babylon. It is also conceivable that the "tribe of Cush" migrated from Mesopotamia to Ethiopia—the Semitic tribes of South Arabia who crossed into Africa and became Abyssinians began their long migration from the same place, Mesopotamia. Ethiopian Professor Hable Selassie is one of many scholars who suggest that his country's Hamitic and Semitic peoples both migrated by way of Yemen, and Professor Taddesse Tamrat stated that Ethiopia depended entirely on southern Arabia for both cultural and economic development. But these two African scholars recognize that a country's development cannot be explained along racial lines.

According to a post-Biblical Jewish tradition, Ham's son Cush[4] was black-skinned as a punishment for his father's sins. In this tale, Ham allegedly had had sexual intercourse in the Ark, and when he saw that Noah was drunk, he emasculated him. Ham was also said to have committed sodomy on his father.

In yet another version, Ham himself was not black, nor were his immediate descendants, including Cush and his son Nimrod.

One Jewish tradition relating to the Sin of Ham— which must offend modern readers—says that the "descendants of Ham have red eyes, because Ham looked upon the nakedness of his father; they have misshapen lips, because Ham spoke with his lips to his brothers about the unseemly

---

[4]In modern Hebrew, blacks are called *cushim*.

condition of his father; and they go about naked, because Ham did not cover the nakedness of his father." According to the legend, another consequence of the curse was that the Egyptians and Ethiopians were led away naked into captivity and exile after they were conquered by the same Assyrian armies that deported the ten tribes of Israel in 722 BCE.[5]

The tribes and Ham shared a similar fate: "Are you not as the children of the Ethiopians are to me, O children of Israel?" it says in Amos. The Soncino Bible's interpretation is that "Degenerate Israel [the ten tribes] is no more to God than the despised inhabitants of distant Ethiopia, the descendants of Ham."

The Christian rationale for the slave trade was based on a conception that the blacks had been damned with the "Curse of Canaan." But while Jews also believed that Ham's descendants were cursed, they never used the legend to justify slavery. Perhaps this was because the Jews themselves had been slaves—and their masters had been *Hamites*, the Egyptians. In the Talmud, there is a tradition that when the Messiah comes and the world offers him gifts, Egypt's gift will at first be rejected, while Ethiopia's offering will be accepted—because Ethiopia was never Israel's taskmaster.

Although some scholars have praised the "scientific accuracy" underlying the Genesis ethnology of the earth's peoples, others, like Dubois, have reacted angrily: "The mixture of blood among the three races is always referred to as an explanation of the advance among negroes and the

---

[5]Eight years after Sennacherib captured Samaria, he marched on Judea, but he interrupted this campaign to move against Ethiopia, conquering this "pearl of all countries."

retrogression among whites. Is this scientific? When a black Jew boasts to his fellow religionists 'I am black but comely, O ye daughters of Jerusalem,' he is supposed to be tanned; when Syria and Arabia show in hair and color their Negro blood, this is completely ignored and their culture called 'white.'" But Dubois was also guilty of ignorance about race—and about the Bible. He simplistically divided the world into three races at a time when anthropologists were challenging most of the popularly held conceptions about race. Modern scholarship has identified a multitude of races—four in East Africa alone. The races inhabiting the East African Rift are called the Mediterraneans, Sudanese, East Africans and Bantus. The ancient Israelites were Mediterraneans, considered a caucasoid group. The Jews of today reflect a spectrum of many races and can no longer be classified as Mediterranean. And the Ethiopians, like all people, borrowed from other cultures: Ethiopia derived its Coptic religion from Egypt (where a black dynasty once ruled) and from Israel, and its language comes from Arabia.

The country of the mixing of races was referred to in 1500 BCE by the remarkable Egyptian Pharaoh Akhnaton, father of child King Tutankhamen. Akhnaton, who may have been the first to introduce a form of monotheism to the world, wrote of Cush in his *Hymn to the Sun*: "In the hills from Syria to Cush and the plain of Egypt, you give everyone his place, and you frame their lives . . . Their tongues are diverse in their speech, their natures in the color of their skin. As a divider, you divide the strange people."

Akhnaton's geographical references define the heart of

the five-thousand-mile-long crack in the earth called the Great Rift. It cleaves the Middle East from Africa at an average width of thirty-five miles with extensive volcanism along its entire length, producing such mountains as Kilimanjaro and Mt. Sinai, and the dramatic topography of the central Ethiopian plateau and the Jordan Valley. It formed Lake Tana, "Jewel of Ethiopia," and determined the rising and sinking of the River of Egypt, the Nile. The Sinai Peninsula holds together two great continents, which still share a great deal in common. The Great Rift highlands of Ethiopia with their deep gorges and tablelands, lakes and mountain chains, also determine the climate along the Red Sea and down the Indian Ocean to Madagascar. Hot desert winds from the dry Middle East sweep down the rift and bring the dry season to East Africa. Caravans have plied the length of the Great Rift for thousands of years. Phoenician ships manned by Israelite sailors stopped at the ports of the Horn of Africa. Whole populations migrated up and down the channel between Asia and Africa.

One thousand years after Akhnaton's rule, in 500 BCE, Herodotus also mentioned the Land of the Burnt Faces as a country of different races, including "negroids from the south and mongoloids from the east." Herodotus called all of the Cushites Ethiopians, as did other Greek writers of antiquity.

LANGUAGE IS another clue to the Falashas' origins. Ethiopians of today speak either Cushitic languages or Semitic tongues, which comprise two of the five sub-families in the Afro-Asiatic language group, and Ethiopian languages are an important link in the chain of Semitic languages. Most Beta-Israel tribesmen used to be bilingual, speaking the Cushitic language of the Agaw as well as the Semitic Amharic or Tigrean tongues. But today only a few Falashas in Qwara, Semien and on the northern fringes of Lake Tana still speak an Agaw dialect. The Ethiopian liturgical language, Ge'ez, is a perfect example of the conglomeration called Ethiopia—it is a combination of a southern Arabian language and the Cushitic language of the Agaw, developed between the fifth and seventh centuries, according to semitist Wolf Leslau.

The Abyssinians—the Amhara and Tigre—call the blacker, more Cushitic Ethiopians *baria* or *shangalla,* meaning slave. The Abyssinians emphasize their Semitic origins—in the past, it was used as a rationale for their domination of the more negroid Ethiopians, the "children of Ham."

In Ethiopia, the blacksheep son of Noah is memorialized in the name of the famous monastery of Debra-Libanos, located at a site in Shoa province called Ham. In the Middle Ages, Beta-Israel blacksmiths were deported to Ham and forcibly converted there.

Intermixing was not a one-sided affair, Dubois and many other scholars have said. It took place in both directions—the Arab Yemenites and the Egyptians, for example, are much darker, more Cushitic, than the Arabs of Lebanon and Syria. And the Yemenite Jews acquired the same physical characteristics as their Arab-African neighbors—an obvious consequence of the fact that Ethiopian troops once occupied South Arabia, while at other times the

South Arabians controlled Ethiopia. Yet it remains a difficult concept for some people to grasp—there are black Jews.

Like the Falashas, the B'nei Israel—Jews of India—also acquired the same physical characteristics as their neighbors.

When most of the Indian Jews started immigrating to Israel a generation ago, they ran into trouble: The rabbinical authorities blocked their marriages, asserting that there had been obvious intermarriage in India, since the B'nei Israel are a beetle-dark brown. As one dissenting Israeli Supreme Court justice pointed out when the same treatment was accorded to a Falasha in 1968, there has been just as much intermarriage—and rape, and improper conversion—among Western Jews as among the Asian and African Jews, but immigrants from America or Rumania never ran into the same problems with the Rabbinate as did the dark Jews. For years, a handful of Israeli politicians and religious leaders blocked all efforts to recognize the Beta-Israel as Jews. Many of these people were not acting out of prejudice, but a few important leaders were definitely motivated by their bias that no black—a child of Ham—could also be a Jew, a descendant of Shem, a son of Moses.

Moses in Ethiopia

KING SOLOMON was not the first Jewish leader whose life was entwined with an Ethiopian queen. According to Jewish legend, Moses reigned as king of Ethiopia and married the queen of that country. It was after his flight as a fugitive from Egypt and before his return to lead the Jews to the Promised Land.

War was raging between Ethiopia and Asian nations when Moses appeared, a twenty-seven-year-old man on the run, who had fled Egypt after killing an overseer of Jewish slaves. He became a favorite of King Kikanos and commander of the Ethiopian army. When the king died, Moses succeeded him, married the king's widow, Adoniah, and ruled for forty years. But Moses would not consummate his marriage, for he honored Abraham's injunction: "Thou shalt not take a wife of the daughters of the Canaanites among whom I dwell," as well as Isaac's warning not to "ally thyself by marriage with any of the children of Ham, for the Lord our God gave Ham, the son of Noah, and all his seed as slaves to the children of Shem and Japhet forever."

After forty years,[1] the queen finally told her people that Moses had never had sexual relations with her or honored the gods of Ethiopia. Thus he was forced to give up his throne and leave Ethiopia. Fearing to return to Egypt, Moses went to live among the Medianites. At the same water well where Jacob had met Rachel, Moses met Zipporah, his future wife. She was the daughter of the priest Jethro, the Kenite. In Numbers, it is mentioned that Moses married an "Ethiopian woman" and that his sister Miriam and brother Aaron were critical of the match. The old rabbinical sources maintained that the Ethiopian wife was the same as the Medianite, whose nomad progeny—the

---

[1]Just as Moses ruled Ethiopia for forty years, and Israel in the Wilderness for forty years, so, the Beta-Israel believe, will the Messiah reign forty years in Jerusalem and forty years in Ethiopia.

Kenites—became the Judaized tribe of nomad smiths in Israel and Arabia. And perhaps in Ethiopia too.

Josephus, the first century Jewish historian, recorded a different version of the story of Moses in Ethiopia: Moses went into Ethiopia not as a fugitive, but at the head of an Egyptian army, and captured all of the country except for Saba—Sheba, or Yemen—across the Red Sea. Tharbis, the Ethiopian king's daughter, fell in love with Moses, who promised to marry her if she procured the surrender of Saba, a deed she was eventually able to accomplish. And Moses kept his promise.

The Ethiopians share the legend of Moses with the Jews. According to a manuscript in the National Library of Addis Ababa, Moses was in Egypt when war broke out between that country and Ethiopia. The Ethiopians, who were the aggressors, decided to divert the waters of the Nile by building a dam across the Tekkaze River (which eventually became the traditional boundary of the Falasha kingdom.) Pharaoh was advised by his ministers—a jealous, conniving lot—to send the court favorite, Moses, at the head of an army against the Ethiopians. Moses accepted command of two hundred thousand men, defeated the Ethiopian armies and destroyed the dam across the Tekkaze, the main tributary of the Blue Nile. After he concluded a peace treaty with the Ethiopian ruler and married his daughter, he returned to Egypt. Shortly afterward, Moses broke with Pharaoh and became leader of the Jewish people.

One of the most important rulers in Ethiopia's history was Lalibela, the 12th-century Christian Agaw, who was among the immediate successors of a Falasha queen who ruled northern Ethiopia. Lalibela told Abu Salih, a Moslem

visitor to his court, that his family—the Zagwe dynasty—
was "of the family of Moses and Aaron, on account of the
coming of Moses in Abyssinia, where he married the king's
daughter." Numbers 12 was then cited to the traveler:
Moses had taken an Ethiopian wife. Lalibela said his
clansmen were the progeny of that union. Although this
claim is dismissed by scholars as a pure invention—one
aimed at legitimizing the rebel Zagwe dynasty's overthrow
of the Solomonic line—Abu Salih apparently accepted
Lalibela's story as an explanation for the monarch's physical
appearance: "He was white, and red of complexion, with red
hair," he wrote.

THE BETA-ISRAEL have a particular reverence for Moses,
as exemplified in their moving liturgical story, *The Death of
Moses.*

Some scholars say that this work came to the Falashas
from Arab tradition, and they point out the Moslem touches
to the story. But Wolf Leslau, who translated *The Death of
Moses* into English, suggests that the Christian and Moslem
legends "may very well stem from Jewish sources." It seems
to be a Jewish story:

Moses is visited by the Angel of Death. He goes up
Mount Sinai to pray to God and read the Torah. God tells
him: "When exile, hunger, abundance, joy, sickness, poverty and sorrow arrive, those who deny Me will be brought
to the fires of hell." Believers will be rewarded, while the
ungrateful wealthy are dragged to Gehenna, along with
those who sin laughing. God says: "I shall not show them
mercy."

Then Moses asked God: When will I die? God made

Moses the exception among men and told him: "I shall take thy soul away on Friday."

Moses wore his burial clothes, and when the day came, the Angel of Death appeared before him, "a young man of the children of Israel"; Moses' knees trembled and he fell on his face. "Hearken Moses, I am the one who is tasted by women and children, the one who destroys houses and builds graves until the coming of the end of the world. I am Suryal, the Angel of Death."

Moses asked for a few more hours, till three in the morning, so he could take leave of his wife and children. And Death waited and "sat shaded from the sun." Moses collapsed pale and wretched at his wife's door. She asked him if he had lost his wealth, his camels and gold. "Who calls me but God, and who frightens me but Death?" he said. She cried, awakened the sleeping children and told them: "Go to your father before he dies, for you shall see him no more. Look well at your father until you be satisfied, for soon you will be parted." All of them wept. Moses placed his younger son, Eleazar, on his right knee and Gershom, the elder son, on his left knee and blessed them.

God asked Moses why he was crying, and he answered that he was worried about his family, for his wife's father, Jethro, was dead, and so was his brother Aaron. God then gave Moses the power "to smite the sea" and he broke open a big rolling stone. Inside the stone, a small worm eating grass said: "Blessed be God, who did not forget me until this day, while I was in the depths of the sea." God assured Moses that his children would be secure. Then God told Moses to get ready.

He embraced his family and walked from the house,

losing his way. He met three men digging a grave, and he helped them—they were three angels. Moses then entered the grave and met the Angel of Death: "Peace upon thee, Moses, son of Amran . . ."

The text of this work *The Death of Moses,* is read at the grave during every Beta-Israel funeral.

The Gold of Sheba

THE MOST celebrated liaison between Ethiopian and Jew is recorded in the Bible—a few brief lines, in First Kings, tells the story of Solomon and Sheba's queen. The Abyssinians— Amhara and Tigre tribes—trace their origins to Menelik, the product of the one-night affair between Israel's king and a queen of Ethiopia, while some Beta-Israel and Agaw tribesmen share a tradition that they are descended from Solomon and one of the queen's ladies-in-waiting, whose son was named Zage.

The Biblical story of Solomon and Sheba is considered to be historical by Christians and Jews, and richly embellished variations are found in Jewish, Moslem and Ethiopian writings. Historian John Bright and archeologist William F. Albright are among many scholars who believe that the Queen of Sheba's visit to Solomon is grounded in historical fact. The three-thousand-year-old tale from the Golden Age of Solomon has captured the imagination of poets, philosophers, even oilmen—Wendell Phillips, once the biggest oil tycoon in the world, discovered Marib, the Queen of Sheba's city, during a 1962 expedition in Yemen. For Sheba, or Saba, is usually identified as South Arabia, which was linked with and sometimes unified with Ethiopia through many centuries.

The Queen of Sheba decided to go to Jerusalem after hearing of King Solomon and the God of the Jews, according to the Biblical account. She traveled with a great retinue: camels laden with spices, precious stones, and an enormous quantity of gold. The queen also had some riddles—"hard questions"—to test the king's mettle. Apparently Solomon gave her all the right answers, for "there was nothing hidden from the King." The queen was awed by Solomon's court and by the splendor of the Temple. She had heard of his wisdom and glory, "but the half was not told me . . . Blessed be the Lord your God, who delighted in you and set you on the throne of Israel; because the Lord loved Israel forever, he has made you king . . ." Then she gave him four and one half tons of gold as a gift, as well as a huge quantity of precious spices.

At this point in the story, the Biblical writer appears to digress suddenly to mention in a few words that King Hiram of Tyre's navy brought gold from Ophir and sandalwood and jewels to be used in the building of the Temple. The Sheba story, interrupted by this short verse, then concludes: "And King Solomon gave to the Queen of Sheba all her desire, whatever she asked besides what Solomon gave her of his royal bounty. So she turned, and went back to her own land, she and her servants."

That's the whole story, although there is a slightly different recounting in Chronicles. But there is much more: "She came to Solomon" uses a verb which in Biblical Hebrew often connotes sexual relations, and Jewish tradition interpreted the phrase "Solomon gave her all her desires" to mean that he impregnated her.

The queen gave Solomon one hundred and twenty talents of gold—a gift that shows her country was probably rich in gold deposits. Some writers suggest that the "digression" about King Hiram's ships bringing gold from Ophir was simply the result of a Biblical editor's attempt to include mention of the second major source for gold used to complete the Temple—altogether, six hundred and sixty talents of gold, about fifty thousand pounds, were used in the Temple, which was finished around the middle of the tenth century BCE. But Ophir may have simply been the name of Sheba's gold-bearing region, and the ancient editor's "insertion" may have meant that *all* of the Temple's gold came from Sheba. Many scholars have identified Ophir with Ethiopia, specifically with the Horn of Africa opposite Yemen. The Horn was called Afar, a name similar to Ophir.[1]

Solomon's commercial enterprises helped pay for the gold, silver and wood used in the Temple. His Phoenician allies were partners in Solomon's far-flung trade empire. King Hiram's sailors included many Jews of the tribe of Dan, whose Red Sea stops included "Sheba and Ophir"— Yemen and Ethiopia. The tribe of Dan is linked by rabbis to the Beta-Israel Jews of Ethiopia and perhaps this connection began around Solomon's time, during the gold trade between Sheba and Israel—commerce that was alluded to by the Prophet Joel, as well.

But the tale of Solomon and Sheba provides any number of tangents and digressions. James B. Pritchard, editor of the definitive book on the subject, commenting on the slight changes between the two Biblical accounts, wrote:

---

[1]The Afar tribe still lives in the region, and Ethiopia remains a source of fine gold.

"The tale had already begun the meandering course it was to take through the centuries."

Josephus does not mention Sheba in his *Antiquities*, but a "woman Queen of Egypt and Ethiopia" who was both "philosophically inquisitive" and beautiful to look at. After witnessing Solomon's grandeur, she comes to "esteem the Hebrew people." Josephus called her Nikaule and mentioned the link between Arabians and Ethiopia.

The contention that the Queen of Sheba and her retinue traveled fourteen hundred miles from southern Arabia to Jerusalem is not difficult to accept: in this century, many Jews from Yemen made their way on foot to the Land of Israel. Caravan routes between the two countries are known to have existed for thousands of years. Archeological evidence has shown that Sheba/Saba was a wealthy land, supported by the trade in myrrh and frankincense, much of which was destined for Solomon's kingdom.

A SQUALID, magical bird plays a curious role in later writings about Solomon and Sheba—the hoopoe. It has seen it all on its flight along the Asian-African trail. Israel, and the Great Rift as a whole, shape a major migratory route for birds, and the hoopoe, which is also found in southern Arabia and in the Ethiopian highlands, proliferates from Dan to Beersheba. It has an unmistakable semi-circular crest, cinnamon-speckled plummage, and filthy habits. In flight, the hoopoe, which is listed in the Bible among the unkosher birds, spreads its barred black and white wings, crying "hoo, hoo, hoo." In Ethiopia, the hoopoe can be found north of Lake Tana, in the region inhabited by the Beta-Israel. The Falashas laugh lightheartedly about this bird.

The hoopoe is a harbinger of spring in Israel, and legends about the bird carry strong sexual connotations.[2] In Jewish tradition, the hoopoe was sentenced to death by King Solomon for refusing to come to a banquet—a feast held for all of the kings of the East and the West, as well as for "the wild beasts, the birds, the reptiles, the devils, the demons and the spirits." But as the hoopoe was about to be sentenced, the clever bird diverted Solomon's wrath by telling of his journey to a wealthy country whose main product was frankincense. The hoopoe's tale of the 'kingdom of Kitor' ruled by 'Queen Sheba' aroused Solomon's many interests, according to the ancient Jewish novella called the *Targum Sheni*. Islamic tradition also mentions that the king's sexual and mercantile interests were awakened by the gossipy report of his hoopoe, named Yafur, who had brought him a "message from Sheba." Yafur had toured Sheba accompanied by the queen's hoopoe, Afir.

In the Jewish tradition, the queen is portrayed as beautiful but hairy—a demon covered in hair. A depilatory had to be concocted for her to remove the hair before Solomon could "lie with her." The result of their union was Nebuchadnezzar—not Menelik—the Babylonian king who would destroy the Temple built by his "father" (or, his progenitor, since he lived some four hundred years after Solomon's reign) and who would take the Jews of Judea into captivity.

Cabbalists of the Middle Ages said that the Queen of

---

[2]Israelis sing a song about the golden bird, with lyrics taken from Bialik's poem, rich in sexual imagery: the hoopoe, perched on a palm tree between the rivers of the Fertile Crescent, is a messenger sent out by Solomon to "bring me my lover." The hoopoe also has a sexual role in Islamic East Africa: he is called *hodi* in Swahili, meaning, "May I come in?"

Sheba's acceptance of the Lord of Israel was not sincere and that she reverted to her evil nature. They noted that when Nebuchadnezzar stripped the Temple, he took back the one hundred and twenty talents of gold that his "mother" had brought to Solomon. Thus the queen is seen as a great source of torment for the Jewish people, and the medieval Jewish stories about the Queen of Sheba became studies in demonology: her hairy feet, and her asking of riddles, like the Sphinx, were signs that she was Lilith—the demons' queen who is diphtheria incarnate, strangling infants in their cradles. Lilith is also a succubus; in the Bible, where she is mentioned only once, she is listed among the beasts of prey and spirits that will devastate the land on the Day of Vengeance.

Gershom Scholem cites portions of the *Zohar,* the classic of Cabbalistic works, which interpret the secret of the gold of Sheba: The demonical queen will lay waste Rome at the end of days, while the Messiah, with an amulet made from the gold of Sheba, will rebuild Jerusalem.

Christians of the Middle Ages had the opposite image of the Queen of Sheba: She was portrayed as the Bride of Christ, the Church itself.

In Ethiopia, the Sheba story is the national epic, set forth in the *Kebra Nagast* (Glory of the Kings). The 14th-century work, which is Ethiopia's Bible, is based on an ancient oral tradition that portrays the queen as a virgin who is seduced and impregnated by the devious king of Jerusalem.

The *Kebra Nagast* combines Jewish and Moslem versions of the Solomon and Sheba story with Ethiopian-Christian elements to portray Ethiopia as the "second Zion," sole possessor of the Throne of David and the Divine

Presence. The object was to prove that the Ethiopians had replaced the Jews as the Chosen People. The Ethiopians called the Queen of Sheba "Makeda," and identified her with the New Testament queens—the Queen of the South, and Candace, Queen of the Ethiopians—fusing them into a Christian version of the original Jewish story.

According to the *Kebra Nagast,* Solomon had sent messages to merchants all over the world asking for gold, silver and building materials to erect the House of God. The Temple was being built to house the Ark of the Lord, which was the visible symbol of God's presence and a sign of the covenant between the Jews and God. The king sent one of his messages to Tamrin, the rich Ethiopian merchant, asking for products from Arabia: red gold, sapphires and black wood that could not be eaten by worms. Tamrin took these things to Solomon, and when he returned to Ethiopia he told his queen of the splendors of Solomon's court. As in the Jewish and Moslem traditions, the Ethiopians also emphasized that the trade links between Israel and Ethiopia/ Yemen had been established even before the queen paid her celebrated visit: she traveled along a well-beaten caravan path to visit King Solomon.

In Jerusalem, Queen Makeda learned about the God of Israel from the king of the Jews and decided to abandon the worship of the sun, the stars and the trees. Besides converting her, Solomon was also interested in seducing the beautiful queen. And he tricked her into sleeping with him.

"That night, Solomon had a dream in which the sun departed from Israel and shone brilliantly over Ethiopia forever," the *Kebra Nagast* says. This was the light of the Divine Presence that surrounds the Holy Ark. Solomon gave Makeda a ring and many gifts and bid her farewell, the book says.

Back in her own country, the queen gave birth to Menelik,[3] who eventually learned who his father was. When he grew up he determined to visit Solomon in Jerusalem. The queen gave her son the ring that Solomon had given her and a letter, asking Solomon to send her part of the curtain of the Ark of the Covenant so that it could be worshipped in Ethiopia.

Menelik, who looked like his father, was well received in Jerusalem, where he spent some time studying Jewish laws.

When Menelik decided to return to Ethiopia, Solomon commanded the elders of Israel to send their first-born sons with him to establish a Jewish colony in Ethiopia, and Zadok, the high priest, anointed Menelik king of Ethiopia. As they were about to leave, Menelik and the first-born sons stole the Ark from the Temple and carried it with them to Ethiopia. According to one version of the story, Menelik and twenty Levite priests brought the Ark from Jerusalem across the Red Sea and through Egypt to Makeda's city, the Queen of Sheba's "new Zion" at Axum. This, the Ethiopians say, was how the Divine Presence left Israel and settled in Ethiopia's ancient capital.

The Ethiopian and Jewish traditions about the queen are antithetical, with a reversal of the roles of good and evil.

There are no hoopoes or hairy demonical feet in the *Kebra Nagast*, as in Moslem and Jewish elaborations on the story.

What was the fate of the Ark, another important link between Israel and Ethiopia? In Jewish tradition, the Ark which Moses had ordered built in Sinai to hold the tablets of the Ten Commandments, had a history of wandering

----

[3]"Son of the wise man," from the Arabic.

through the centuries, until the Temple was built to house
it. Before Solomon's time, the Ark was always carried into
battle by the Israelites. It was prohibited to touch the Ark
itself on pain of death. When the Philistines captured it,
they were "smitten with plague"—and they returned the
Ark to the Jews. King David danced before the Ark, but
since he was a man of war, it was left to his son Solomon to
build the Temple to hold the Ark of the Tabernacles. The
Ark was lost to Israel, probably in 586 BCE, when
Nebuchadnezzar and the Babylonians destroyed the Temple.
But it was not included in the list of Temple treasures
carried off by the Babylonians. It was last mentioned in a
mysterious reference in Jeremiah. A legend related in II
Maccabees says that the Ark of the Covenant was concealed
by Jeremiah on Mount Nebo, from which Moses was
allowed to see the Promised Land. Another myth says that
the Ark was hidden in a cave in Jerusalem. But the
Ethiopians claim it was installed in a shrine in Axum, the
"second Jerusalem."

Even in modern times, it was reported that no one was
allowed to enter this shrine except for one monk, who was
assigned for life to the service of the Ark. The Ethiopians say
that the Ark has been moved in times of crisis. In the tenth
century, when the Jewish Queen Yehudit destroyed Axum,
the Ark was sent to Lake Zuway in the south for safekeeping
and brought back to Axum when the city was rebuilt. It was
similarly removed for a time when the Moslems under Iman
Gran almost defeated the Christians in the 16th century.

The Ark is the "pivot round which the Abyssinian
Church revolves," according to Lake Tana explorer R. E.
Cheesman. There is a replica of the Ark, called *tabot,* in every
Ethiopian church, which represents the original Ark of
shittim wood that contained the stone tablets Moses

brought from Mount Sinai. Every year the Christian priests take out the replica ark during the feast of Timkat, or Baptism. As the ark passes, the people prostrate themselves before it. Ethiopian priests, who believe they are the Levites' successors—Falasha priests claim to be the Levites' *descendants*—still dance as David did before the *tabot*. For the legend of the Ark is the cornerstone for the priests' claim that the Ethiopians were the elect of God—in place of the Jews, who had rejected the "messiah"—and, therefore, the Ark was in their custody.

How do the Beta-Israel refer to the Ark? The Ark's power to defeat Israel's enemies is commemorated in one Falasha prayer: "And it came to pass when the Ark set forward that Moses said 'Rise up, Lord, and let Thy enemies be scattered'." And in the *Apocalypse of Baruch*, which is included in the Falasha liturgy, it is related that "God raised up Nebuchadnezzar," who captured Jerusalem, destroyed all its monuments and "captured Zion"—the Ark, whose wood was like a white pearl radiating multicolored images, according to the vision of a 14th century Falasha ascetic, Gorgorios.

One Beta-Israel story, recorded in the 19th century by a Protestant missionary, says that the Christians *did* place the Ark in Axum, but "only when a Falasha approaches it does the wall before it open up, whereupon he prostrates himself in front of the Holy Ark."

The Falashas' belief in the Ark's powers led them to march unarmed to Axum in 1862, where they prayed that the walls of the cathedral holding the Ark would tumble down and they would then take it back to Israel, where it belonged. They were laughed at and beaten, and many of them died on the road.

4

The Great Rift

Dan: The Black Sheep

THE ETHIOPIAN Jews are descended from the lost tribe of
Dan, according to some of Israel's great rabbis, but this view
is rejected totally by secular scholars, who trace the Beta-
Israel's beginnings to other sources. Aescoly alone mentions
six theories regarding the Beta-Israel's Judaic origins. There
is no historical record to prove or to refute any of the theories
about the Falashas' origins; in fact, it is possible to accept
most of them—for there undoubtedly were several periods
when Jewish influence reached Ethiopia both by way of
Egypt and by way of southern Arabia. There was constant
movement along the Great Rift. There were Jewish trade
colonies and military posts; and migration by Israelites and
their kinsmen since the Exodus span the millenia. Most of
the movement was toward the south, and there was Jewish
intermixing with Egyptians, Nubians, South Arabians and
Ethiopians. The Falashas themselves claim that their num-

85

bers were augmented during several *different* periods of history by Jews expelled from Palestine and Arabia.

But the rabbis have fastened on the Dan theory—a rabbinical interpretation that has important implications for the Jewish people. In 1972 Israel's Chief Sephardic Rabbi, Ovadia Yosef, declared in a statement that the Beta-Israel are Jews, "undoubtedly of the Lost Tribe of Dan." He based his decision on the findings of several previous chief rabbis and *gaonim*, geniuses of Jewish law, including the late Chief Rabbi Avraham Kook and the 15th-century Radbaz of Egypt, David Ben Zimra. Ovadia Yosef said that the Falashas are "descendants of Israel's tribes that have gone south to Cush, and I have no doubt that those rabbis who have decided that they are of the Tribe of Dan have investigated and discussed and reached this conclusion relying on reliable evidence . . . I've decided that they are Jews that should be saved from assimilation." The chief rabbi called for their immediate immigration to Israel.

Secular scholars spurn this rabbinical claim. "Rabbi Ovadia Yosef doesn't know what he's talking about," according to Ethiopia scholar Mordechai Abir, a Hebrew University professor. "I had very good friends in Ghana who assured me that they were descended from one of the lost tribes, and they recited a whole history—their people got it from the missionaries in the 19th century, they got it all mixed up with Christianity and animism. The Falashas are simply a Cushitic people who accepted some part of Jewish beliefs. I say they are converts of converts."

THERE WERE twelve tribes of Israel descended from

Abraham, Isaac and Jacob, who was also called Israel: Judah, Dan, Reuben, Gad, Naphtali, Issachar, Benjamin, Simeon, Levi, Asher, Zevulun; and Joseph's two sons, Manasseh and Ephraim, who formed half tribes. These sons were the forefathers of the Jews.

Dan was Jacob's fifth son and the first child of Bilah, Rachel's maid. He came to be regarded as "the black sheep of the House of Jacob," perhaps from the time he plotted against the life of his brother Joseph. When Jacob was dying, he gave his blessings to his sons. Jacob said of Dan: "He shall be a serpent by the way." Thereafter, the tribe of Dan's battle standard contained a serpent.

The Danites worshipped idols during the time of the Exodus. Nevertheless, the tribe was entrusted with the holy task of helping to build the Ark of the Tabernacles in the Sinai. Dan became the second biggest tribe after Judah and was known for its prowess in war—its most famous son would be the hero Samson.

When the Jews entered Israel, the land was divided among the tribes. Much of what is called the Dan Region in modern Israel—the Tel Aviv area southeast to Beit Shemesh—was given to Jacob's "black sheep."

As mentioned earlier, during King Solomon's reign, the Danites hired themselves out as sailors to Phoenician shipowners. King Hiram of Tyre was a close ally of Solomon's, and the Israelites took part in the booming trade on the Red Sea-Indian Ocean route. So the Danite sailors must have been familiar with the Jewish trade colonies that extended all along this route, including, probably, ports in Eritrea and all along the Horn of Africa.

Several hundred years after the twelve tribes had captured the Holy Land, and shortly after Solomon's death, ten of the tribes split from Judah and Benjamin in a furious dispute. The ten tribes formed the northern Kingdom of Israel, while the Jewish state in the south was called Judah. This Great Schism that was "destined" to come about—God said "for this thing is from me"—was led by Jeroboam, who defied the decree which had made Jerusalem's Temple the sole site for proper worship of God. The ten tribes that followed Jeroboam set up rival centers of worship at Dan and Bethel, engaging in paganistic practices that, according to the Bible, eventually brought divine retribution. That came when they were captured by the Assyrians in 722 BCE and erased from history.

The tribe of Dan was among the Israelites carried off by Sargon to Assyria and the cities of the Medes, where they vanished. Only a legend remained: ten of the twelve Jewish tribes were swallowed in the rift, but they did not perish. The belief persisted that they would be recovered, despite the gravity of Israel's sin—idolatry. "And the Lord rejected all the seed of Israel and afflicted them, and delivered them into the hands of spoilers, until he cast them out of his sight," Second Kings relates. But prophecy kept the legend of the lost tribes alive, especially the passage from Isaiah that said the Lord would "recover the remnant of His people" from Assyria (Syria), Cush (possibly Ethiopia) and the ends of the earth, and the prophecy of Ezekiel that all the tribes will join with Judah to form a single realm.

Josephus, in the period of the Second Temple, said the lost tribes represented an "immense multitude." But there was one very important dissenter—nineteen hundred years ago, Rabbi Akiba said "the ten tribes shall not return again."

Some two hundred years after the catastrophe that befell the Kingdom of Israel in 722 BCE, the two surviving tribes of the Kingdom of Judah were themselves exiled when the Babylonians destroyed Solomon's Temple. Judah and Benjamin survived the long captivity in Babylon, while no one knew the fate of the Israelites who earlier had been brought to the same area by the Assyrians. Jews continued to believe that their lost brethren were in a kind of limbo, exiled beyond the mysterious river called Sambatyon.

One report, by the ninth-century traveler Eldad Hadani, claimed that the tribe of Dan left Israel even before the Assyrian conquest, choosing to go into exile rather than follow Jeroboam in his rebellion against Solomon's son, Rehoboam, and in his apostasy.

The ancient Assyrian empire encompassed an area from Israel to India and included Babylon, but as the legends of the lost tribes grew, so did the number and variety of their geographical locations. There were claims that the lost Israelites had become the Japanese, the Tartars, American Indians, Chinese, Bantus, Dutch, Greeks and Russians. In 1644, a Jew named Aaron Levi de Montezinos claimed that he had met Indians in South America who recited the *Shma Yisrael* prayer: "Hear O' Israel, the Lord is our God, the Lord is One." And his report inspired a book, *Hope of Israel*, which in turn influenced Oliver Cromwell to permit the Jews to return to England. There are other tomes which set out to prove that the Afghans, Kurds, Mongols and Khazars are Israelites, and a recent tract theorized that the tribe of Dan became the Greeks. In the United States, fundamentalist churches claim the English and Americans are direct descendants of Israel's lost tribes. But in Colonial America, Roger Williams, William Penn and Cotton Mather all identified the Indians with the Jews: "When I look at their children, I imagine myself in the Jewish Quarter of London," Penn wrote.

Everywhere, there seem to be strange pockets of people who are identified as "lost Jews"—the Quechuan Indians in the Andes, or the colony of "Jewish Indians" near the town of Pachuca, in Mexico. In Africa, the Nubas of Sudan, the Masai of Kenya, and the Zulus and Kaffirs of South Africa were labeled as lost tribes by the missionaries. There are other Ethiopian tribes besides the Falashas that claim kinship with the Jews—but their legends are not connected with the ten lost tribes. (Several tribes in East Africa besides the Ethiopians show that they were once heavily influenced by Judaism. These include the Wakalindi of Kenya and the Sakalavas of Madagascar, who may have acquired some of their customs and beliefs from the Israelite adventurers and merchants traveling the Red Sea route to Arabia and East Africa.)

It has been remarked that some of those who are most intent on tracing the ten lost tribes are Jews seeking their own origins, or who want, perhaps, to reaffirm the uniqueness of Judaism and Jewish history. Apostate Jews have also been among the most fervid seekers of the lost tribes. In the 19th century, several German-Jewish converts to Christianity became fanatical missionaries and searched out Jewish sects in the most remote areas of the world. Henry Stern, who preached to the Falashas, was one of these lapsed Jews, as was Dr. Joseph Wolff, who sought to convert "kinsmen" whom he found living with the Uzbeck Tartars. He found other "lost Jews" at Poona, India, who called themselves B'nei Israel, or Sons of Israel. And he discovered that the fifteen thousand Bokhara Jews—and Moslem Afghans as well—also preferred to call themselves B'nei Israel.[1]

The various B'nei Israel sects found in Iran, India, Turkey, Afghanistan and southern Russia are in areas contiguous with the ancient Assyrian empire, where the ten tribes were exiled. But some scholars, like Allen Godbey, maintain that the notion of the lost tribes is myth, saying that these Sons of Israel clusters represent only the descendants of colonies of Jews established in trading posts by King Solomon. Godbey maintains that they have Jewish origins, but they are not lost tribes—and this, he claims, is also true of the Falashas.

The Falashas themselves will tell you many ancient stories about their origins, and "the lost tribe of Dan" is only one of them. There seems to be some truth to them all.

The Island of Elephantine

WHEN HERODOTUS wrote in the fifth century BCE of the Jewish settlement at Elephantine, the Nile island on the ancient border between Egypt and Nubia, the jungle

---

[1]In modern times, most of the Indian and Bokharian Jews have immigrated to Israel.

outpost already had a long and rich history. Elephantine, where the Nile passes the granite barrier of the First Cataract, near the modern city of Aswan, was for centuries the site of a major armed camp, with a large contingent of Jewish mercenaries. They arrived there with the Persians, who carried away thousands of Jews to fight in various parts of the Persian empire. Cambyses of Persia encouraged Jewish settlement in Egypt, and himself marched into Ethiopia, taking Jewish soldiers with him. Jewish civilians—merchants and traders—joined the Elephantine community, for it soon became the center of thriving commerce with Nubia and Ethiopia, especially in ivory.

The Elephantine Jews built a temple—the first outside Jerusalem since the Great Schism—in contravention of the Jewish religion. This temple was described in Egyptian papyri from the fifth century BCE. Historian Cyrus Gordon, in an attempt to explain this heterodoxy, said that the Elephantine Jews came from enclaves in Syria which had been cut off from Judea during the Great Schism that brought the breakup of Solomon's empire. This would also explain the community's ignorance of Hebrew and of later developments in Judaism. It is not remarkable that the Ethiopian Jews, who were even more remote than the Jews of the Upper Nile, knew nothing of Hebrew or post-Mosaic Judaism, and that they adopted strange customs.

Several scholars have suggested that the Falashas may have been converted by Israelites from Elephantine. The late Israeli President Ben-Zvi, in an article on Jewish tribes in Arabia, also said that the Beta-Israel came from the Elephantine garrison. According to the *Encyclopedia of*

Religion and Ethics, the Elephantine Jews were descendants of the Northern Israelites, which includes the tribe of Dan.

The theory that the Falashas were converted by the Elephantine Jews is dismissed by Ethiopia scholar Edward Ullendorff. "A dispassionate appraisal of the ethnic and religious position of the Falashas places them squarely into the mainstream of Ethiopian life," he states emphatically. The Falashas are simply "descendants of elements in the Axumite Kingdom who resisted conversion to Christianity." They are "not a lost tribe of Israel," but "adherents to fossilized Hebraic-Jewish beliefs." Allen Godbey held a similar view: "The distinctive features of the Falashas' religion point to a pre-exilic time, when Solomon's Temple was in high repute . . . They are simply Judaized Agaw." But while Ullendorff believes the Jewish influence in Ethiopia came by way of South Arabia, Godbey claimed that it came by way of Egypt, where there were Jewish colonies even before Elephantine—during Isaiah's time, about 700 BCE.

What is striking about Elephantine is the fact that a Jewish colony existed for hundreds of years near the heart of black Africa, thousands of miles from Jerusalem but only five hundred miles from the Tekkaze River of Ethiopia, the northern border of the once independent Falasha kingdom. The people of Elephantine were the earliest known explorers of inner Africa and the southern Red Sea. According to Zephaniah, there were Jewish colonies even *beyond* "the rivers of Nubia."

The traders ventured inland to obtain Ethiopia's treasures. Elephants (valued for their ivory and for use in war), rhinoceros horn (still considered an aphrodisiac), hippopotamus hides, apes, tortoise shells, gold, myrrh, frankincense, ginger, cassia and cinnamon were mentioned by the Roman historian, Pliny. Jews were among the "caravan conductors" who brought Pharaoh the ivory tusks and spices from "barbarian" lands.

The Falashas lived along the Tekkaze, whose Great Rift valleys were rich in elephants, and northern Ethiopia was a caravansary for traders in search of ivory and the tanks of the ancient world. They were joined by Jewish mercenaries from garrisons like Elephantine, who grew restless and traveled into Ethiopia. Herodotus wrote that the Elephantine warriors, after being stationed on the island without relief, deserted their posts and departed in a body southward, where they offered their services to the Ethiopian king at Meroe. The large number of Jews among the mercenaries (Breasted called them Syrians, but they were Jews from Syria), may have stayed on in Ethiopia.

It seems more than plausible that some of these soldiers intermarried and converted the tribe that came to be called the Falashas.

Many Falashas believe that the tribe came to Ethiopia from Egypt. One version of the story was recorded by anthropologist Michelle Schoenberger, who interviewed the Falashas' high priest in 1972:

"The Falashas migrated like many of the other sons of Israel to Egypt and exile after the destruction of the First Temple by the Assyrians in 586 BC.[1] This group of people was led by the great priest, On."

[1]The Babylonians, not the Assyrians, destroyed the Temple.

[A Jewish temple and colony existed at On-Heliopolis, which today is a Cairo suburb. The temple, like that at Elephantine was built in defiance of the principle there could only be one Temple—in Jerusalem. This was a basic issue in the ten tribes' split from Judah, and the temples at On and Elephantine were in the tradition of Jeroboam's apostasy at Dan.] The Beta-Israel remained in exile in Egypt for a few hundred years, until the reign of Cleopatra, according to the high priest.

The high priest said that the Jews supported Cleopatra in her war against Augustus Caesar. "When she was defeated, it became dangerous and difficult for the small minorities to remain in Egypt, and so there was another migration [around 35 BCE]. Some of the migrants went to South Arabia and further to Yemen. Some of them went to the Sudan and continued on their way to Ethiopia, helped by Egyptian traders, who guided them through the desert. Some of them entered Ethiopia through Qwara [by way of Sudan] and some came via Eritrea."

[The 19th century missionary J. M. Flad recorded a Falasha tradition that the Ethiopian Jews left Egypt at the time of the Exodus and settled in the province of Qwara. The Tigreans believe that during the Exodus thousands of Jews did not manage to cross the parted waters of the Red Sea in time. They drifted down the shore of the sea until they reached the Abyssinian mountains].

The Beta-Israel settled in Ethiopia before the incursion of the Tigreans, the Amhara and the Galla (Oromo), their high priest continued. "At this time, Ethiopia was populated by indigenous peoples—the Agaw tribes and partly by Semitic Arabian tribes. The population at this time was ignorant of any handicrafts or technology. This made it a very convenient place for the Falashas to settle, for they had come from a civilization in Egypt with a knowledge of craftsmanship, such as building, smithing, weaving and potting. With their knowledge of these crafts, they became the uncrowned governors of the area. They were able to influence the population. Intermarriage followed, because most of the Jewish immigrants were men. And they called themselves Beta-Israel."

In later interviews with the anthropologist the high priest embellished this story, bringing in references to the ten lost tribes and to the disputed fact that the Falashas are members of the tribe of Dan. He was, of course, aware of the developments in Israel, where the Beta-Israel had been recognized as the Danites by Chief Rabbi Ovadia Yosef. His references to Cleopatra do not jibe with historical sources, which portray her as being extremely hostile to the Jews of Alexandria and other Egyptian cities.

5

Asia-Africa Routes

Village Smithy

THERE IS AN ancient, vital clue to the mysterious origins of the black African Jews: The roots of the Beta-Israel may be found by tracing their knowledge of metallurgy, which the tribe claims it introduced to Ethiopia in pre-historic times. This "sorcerers' skill" illuminates the beginnings and inspiration of Ethiopia's Jews, linking Africans and Israelites. Where did the Falashas learn ironsmithing, an epic craft in the history of civilization? The few scholars who touch on the subject hold differing views, often dividing along the same lines as they do over how the Falashas acquired Judaism: either by way of Egypt or by way of Arabia. Others contend that the Beta-Israel learned their metal skills in a totally African environment, or from 16th-century Portuguese soldiers.

There were successive waves of Jewish migration along both legs of the Asia-Africa routes from the time of

Solomon, ca. 1000 BCE, until at least sixteen hundred years later. Jews and Ethiopians were in close contact throughout this period, but one of the most important connections between Jews and the people who came to be called Falashas occurred toward the end of the migrations. It is possible that the Jewish smiths of Yemen—and perhaps some of the nomadic Jewish smiths around the Kheibar oasis as well— were carried off to Ethiopia in 525 CE. It was a watershed year in the history of the region—the Ethiopian Christian monarch, Caleb, destroyed South Arabia's Jewish kingdom, ruled by King Dhu-Nuwas, the son of a Jewish slave who followed his mother's religion. It is known that Caleb brought Jewish captives to his home country, in the Axum-Gondar areas of northwest Ethiopia. It is likely that these slaves were allowed to intermarry with the aboriginal tribes, the Cushitic natives who were gradually being subjugated by the Amhara and Tigre tribes. Perhaps those Jewish smiths who were among the captives taught their metallurgical skills as well as their Judaism to a branch of the Agaw tribe that thereafter called itself Beta-Israel. The tribe's superstitious neighbors called the Falashas, *tayb* (smith), as well as *ayhud* (Jew).

But some obvious, further questions are raised by this theory. Why, for example, did the Beta-Israel learn only Mosaic Judaism—the Pentateuch—and nothing of the Talmudic tradition if they were converted as late as 525, centuries after the Talmud became Jewish law? And it is not only Talmudic lore that the Falashas missed, but Hebrew lore as well. One clue may be found in the existence of other Jewish smith-tribes in neighboring Arabia who were also cut off from the rabbinical developments in Judaism. Most of these nomad tinkers were said to be descendants of the Biblical Kenite smiths, who had intermarried with the Israelites.

Wolf Leslau believes the Beta-Israel are descended from converts whose Jewish mentors came to Ethiopia from Arabia. Leslau, Joseph Halevy and other scholars have noted that the early sixth century was the period when Judaism was sweeping Arabia and Ethiopia. The Beta-Israel's own oral history, as related by their high priest, also indicates that the African-Jewish tribe originated during this period. There is little primary historical evidence available, but King Caleb left some stone inscriptions that indirectly refer to the conquered Jews of Yemen and to the Judaized Africans of Ethiopia. It *is* known that there was a sizable colony of Jewish blacksmiths in Yemen, and that because of their metal skills they were considered sorcerers and were scorned as outcasts by their Arabian neighbors, Christian and pagan alike.

The significant links between the metalsmiths of Arabia and the smiths of Ethiopia include some shared religious beliefs, a pariah social status stemming from their "magic," and their geographical proximity—Jewish Yemenites and Ethiopians were in contact up until 1950, when the Yemenite Jews were taken to Israel. Religious ties are the most important factor, but the metalsmith connection is also significant, even though "secrecy, sexual taboos, the personification of hammer and anvil, and the inheritance of the profession are likely to occur almost anywhere," according to W. Cline in his work on metallurgy in black Africa.

The anti-Semite equates evil with Jew, in Sartre's

analysis, and this has been as true in Africa as it has been in Europe, Asia and the Americas. In Ethiopia today the Beta-Israel are still *buda* to their neighbors because they are Jews and metalworkers—*buda* attributes evil eye/Satan powers to the blacksmith.

The Beta-Israel are singled out by the Amhara, the Tigre and even by the Agaw, their so-called kinsmen, as the main possessors of *buda*. The Ethiopian Jews have for centuries been accused of being cannibalistic hyenas bred in hell. In 1684 the German scholar Job Ludolf heard of the Falashas from his Amhara informant, who said about the blacksmiths: "The silly vulgar people could not endure smiths—the sort of Mortals that spit fire and were bred up in hell." In the 19th century, several English travelers[1] remarked that the Beta-Israel suffered the blood libel because of their ironmaking craft: the Jews turned themselves into hyenas at night, their neighbors said, in order to prey on the blood of Amhara children. This widespread belief persists: The Amhara continue to blame the Jewish tribe in their midst for *buda*-sickness, poisoning souls, possessing young women, and causing blindness, consumption, insanity and death. This is all directly related to blacksmithing and Jews.

Iron technology, the revolutionary skill that transformed civilization everywere, spread down the long valley of the Great Rift, reaching East Africa at a relatively late stage—about the sixth century.

---

[1]Sir Richard Burton, Mansfield Parkyns, Henry Salt, Esq., and William Harris, among others.

The Beta-Israel say that they brought smithing knowledge to Ethiopia, and that they paid an enormous price for revolutionizing the country's agriculture and warfare. They represented a kind of Dracula/Wolfman to the Christians, who believed that a Falasha could take a quantity of ashes, sprinkle them over his shoulder, and undergo an instant metamorphosis. It was claimed that the blacksmith's skin assumed the hair and color of the hyena, while his limbs and head took the shape of that hated animal.

Most of the "possessed" Ethiopians were women. "The reason of their being attacked is often that they have despised the proffered love of some *buda*," an English traveler wrote, noting that "the Devil" was often blamed for the work of "Cupid." The Jews of Gondar province, Semien and Walqayt, are called wizards and cannibals, and in Tigre too, the terms *falasha, buda,* and *tayb* are still used synonymously. The Beta-Israel are blamed for disinterring corpses and turning them into domestic animals—"remarkably fine" mules, for example. Christian Ethiopians have killed Falashas because of this belief. An Adowa man, thinking the corpse of his mother had been turned into an ass, drove a spear through a blacksmith's heart. Elsewhere in Tigre, a soldier possessed by a *buda* named a village smith as his tormentor; and the provincial ruler, after a brief "investigation," ordered the blacksmith and his family thrown into a fiery pit—to the applause of the peasants. This treatment was common until recent times. The stories are still pertinent to the present situation of the Falashas—the *buda* is directly blamed for the crucifixion of Jesus, and the Falasha craftsmen allegedly engineered the deed. "The blacksmith made the nails and the carpenters made the cross. And while Christ hung on the cross, he cursed those people whose skills made it possible to crucify him," according to an Amhara religious belief.

Paradoxically, the metal craft which made the Jews a frequent target for executions also kept them from being totally exterminated, since they monopolized the smelting of ore and the forging of iron into weapons and tools.

But the argument that the Beta-Israel had an exclusive knowledge of metalsmithing is rejected by several scholars. Berkeley anthropologist William Shack, for example, dismisses the claim out of hand, saying that other Ethiopians had metallurgical skills for many centuries, and citing metal objects found at Axum that are seventeen hundred years old. He also pointed out that *buda* is applied to other tribes besides the Beta-Israel, and that the tribe's pariah status is no different than that of other "occupational groups"—the tanners, for example. He said that there have always been non-Falasha blacksmiths among the Ethiopians. But history scholar J. Quirin, who has studied the Beta-Israel's metalsmith occupation and the tribe's pariah caste status, has written that even though other Ethiopians have been called *buda*, there was always a definite *emphasis* on the Jews, and gradually, "the attribute began to be assigned almost exclusively to Beta-Israel blacksmiths and potters." Ironworkers in other parts of Ethiopia, whether or not they are called Falasha, are also called *buda*. This only points to the possibility that many of Ethiopia's other ironsmiths were converted Beta-Israel, descended from Falashas who were dispersed by Ethiopian rulers throughout the Period of the Wars, 1270-1632. The *tabiban* (smiths) undoubtedly were Beta-Israel faced with the option of conversion or execution, and they became the Marranos of Ethiopia. "Royal necessities moved a considerable colony of Falasha smiths to Shoa,[3] and forced upon them a nominal Christianity," Godbey wrote in 1931. "They are still essentially secret Falashas. And they continue their secret worship in their mountain gorges." This contention is supported by Quirin, who also argues that the *tabiban* in Shoa, the heartland of Amhara emperors, "originated from Beta-Israel dispersals," and, he says, those tribesmen who converted to Christianity held on to their Judaic beliefs. He cites Beta-Israel oral traditions and concludes that the Falashas were dispersed to Shoa from the 14th century until the 17th century.

The 16th-century Jesuit Francisco Alvarez noted in his account of the Portuguese expedition to Abyssinia that the Ethiopians' makers of metal weapons and tools always traveled with the royal court, fashioning coats of mail, lances, spears and swords. The smiths were confined to a separate area on the fringe of the royal encampment.

After Yeshaq (reigned 1413-1430) defeated most of the Beta-Israel, he ordered the manufacturing of swords and coats of mail, and the subjugated Falashas became his principal workers. The Ethiopian rulers routinely dispersed the Beta-Israel smiths, enslaved them or killed them. At one point, Zar'a Yacqob (1434-68) exiled Jewish smiths to places as far as Harar in the Ogaden desert, and then ordered

---

[3]Specifically, to Debra Libanos monastery at Ham.

the execution of all his smiths because they practiced "sorcery."

Quirin offers a theory that the Beta-Israel first became blacksmiths, potters and weavers in the 15th century, adopting completely *new* occupations. But even though his study elsewhere relies heavily on Beta-Israel oral history, which he recorded extensively, he dismisses the tribe's assertion that they "have been artisans since their alleged origins in ancient Israel . . . Regardless of that tradition, the combination of military defeat and Yeshaq's desires strongly suggest that the 15th century was critical for their emphasis on ironworking."

Some Falashas, including religious leaders, claim they acquired the skill in 525; others insist that they brought the craft with them from Egypt, long before the sixth century.

Quirin suggested that the Portuguese taught metal-smithing to the Beta-Israel, but there is no evidence for this. In fact, the Portuguese armed the Amhara, and not the Jews, even though the Beta-Israel joined the Christian forces in battle against the Moslems.

Sources on how far back the Falashas' craft skills go are inadequate. But no other smith tribes are mentioned in the Ethiopian medieval chronicles—only *ayhud*, the Jew.

THE ETHIOPIAN rulers of the medieval period were not the first despots to recognize the need for deporting or killing the metalsmiths of a conquered people. This was also the practice of earlier times. The Assyrians, who exiled the ten tribes of Israel and also deported conquered Ethiopians, always made certain that the metalsmiths were the first to go. They were the arms makers, and in addition, the agricultural economies depended on their skills.

The Assyrians used iron on a lavish scale, and weapons, tools and one hundred and fifty tons of unworked iron were found in the palace of Sargon II. Steel was the most revolutionary development in the ancient history of warfare. In 722 BCE, the Assyrians under Sargon deported the Jews of Israel, including the blacksmiths, and Sennacherib took similar action in the following generation when he captured the southern kingdom, Judah. Blacksmiths and metalworkers in Mesopotamia were highly valued. "Sennacherib mentions expressly that he carried off the smiths of Babylon and Nebuchadnezzar did the same with those of Jerusalem," Forbes noted.

Did the smiths of the ten tribes survive Assyrian exile? Herodotus in 500 BCE described the swarthy artisans of Colchis, near an Assyrian outpost on the Black Sea contiguous with Georgia, an area regarded by the ancient Greeks as the special domain of sorcery. These artisans were metalsmiths who circumcised their sons in accord with Mosaic law and who claimed to be descended from refugees of Assyrian oppression.

It is possible that some Jewish smiths survived on the fringes of the empire, and that others settled in countries that the Assyrians penetrated but did not hold. When the Assyrians invaded Egypt and Ethiopia and displaced the black African Twenty-Fifth Dynasty (751-664 BCE) that ruled both countries, Israelite smiths were included in the conqueror's armies. This invasion occurred sixty years after the disappearance of the ten tribes. In 666 BCE the Assyrians, with the help of their superior iron weapons, defeated the Egyptians and Cushites, whose arms were made of bronze or stone.

The defeated Cushites fled south along the rift valley to Meroe, near the Atbara River caravan routes of Abyssinia. Meroe eventually became the biggest ironmaking center in all of Africa, with immense mounds of ore heaped on all sides of the large settlement. The Cushites themselves had originated in Mesopotamia, mixed with the indigenous Ethiopians, and established the Cush Empire with its main cities of Napata and Meroe. Only five hundred miles away, on the island of Elephantine, Jewish smiths had appeared as early as the seventh century BCE. But it is Greek mercenaries who are often credited with teaching ironworking to the inhabitants of Meroe during the fifth century BCE, despite evidence that it was introduced by Jewish craftsmen. How this knowledge reached beyond the *sudd* swamps is another problem.

The skin bellows used by blacksmiths is a key tool in the development of civilization. It came to Africa—and to Europe—from the Middle East, specifically from Mesopotamia, whose highly valued smiths were called *nappahu*. It is significant that the Mesopotamians and Hebrews shared a word for metalworkers—*nappeh* means "user of bellows." It is another indication that Jewish smiths dominated the metal craft in Assyria, Babylonia—and Ethiopia. For it was Semitic tribes that brought the technology of iron to Ethiopia from South Arabia, according to several writers, including Ethiopian historian Sergew Hable-Sellassie. Geographer Frederick Simoons, however, has suggested that the iron plow was used by indigenous highland people in Begembdar and Semien—where most Falashas live—long before the first Semitic invasion of Ethiopia ca. 1000 BCE. It seems to be anybody's guess. There are Egyptian reliefs that picture Asian nomads with blacksmith's tools arriving in the Land of the Nile, indicating that the craft was introduced to Ethiopia via Egypt instead of Arabia.

There are those who reject both theories, viewing them as being inspired by "cultural racism"—and there is no question that advances in African civilization have too often been credited to Semitic Arabs, Caucasian Europeans, or North African and Asian Hamites. There are experts on every side of the issue. In the case of metallurgy, Von Luschan, De Mortillet and Balfour have claimed that the discovery of iron was made in black Africa, and Iron Age sites dating to 500 BCE have been discovered in Tanzania. But such authorities as Forbes and Cline insist that the East Africans, at least, gained their knowledge of ironsmithing from the Middle East. Native Africans did smelt iron ore at an early period, but they borrowed techniques and refinements from migrating Semites—from both Arabia and Egypt.

In an ancient triangular trade between Ethiopia, Egypt and Mesopotamia by way of Israel and Arabia, iron and the craft of metalsmithing became a major element in the pattern of commerce, war, agriculture and migration along the routes of the Great Rift. The first-century Greek merchant who wrote the *Periplus of the Erythryan Sea* took note of the trade in iron tools that Africans imported[4]—mainly from the Himyarite (Yemenite) princes of South Arabia, where Jewish smiths manufactured metal products in Muza, a port city on the Arabian coast only a few miles from Ethiopia.

Smiths moved around. It may have been the search for new mines that led to the migration of the very first smiths when the Iron Age was in its infancy, around 1500 BCE. The iron mines of Tigre Province, where thousands of Falashas live, must have been a natural draw for nomadic smith tribes from southern Arabia. Smiths immigrated to Ethiopia—as the name *falasha* implies—and there are other examples of despised smith castes, in northeast Kenya for example. There is a tradition that the first smith in their country came as an immigrant long ago and married a Masai girl.

For the Jews as for other peoples, iron was viewed as a source of evil, and the smith was feared as a magician. In Hebrew, *charash*, or smith, is also a general term for craftsman—and, for magic. The ancient Israelites retained a strong taboo against working with iron tools, which Josephus said were not used to hew the great stones for the First and Second Temples.[5]

Iron was created to shorten man's days, according to

---

[4]Imported iron bars were used by the Axumites to make spears for use in war and hunting, the *Periplus* writer noted.
[5]King Solomon used a magic worm, the *shamir*, to cut the stones for the Temple—he entrusted the hoopoe to transport the worm, according to tradition.

the Mishnah. The taboo against iron and metalsmiths can be traced back to Genesis. In the Bible, the first worker of iron was Tubalkayin, grandson of Cain. He was "the forger of every cutting instrument of copper and iron."[6] *Kain* in Syriac and Arabic means metalsmith/craftsman, and in Biblical Hebrew, *kain* also means a metal weapon, probably a spear.

The Biblical Cain is considered to be the progenitor of the tribe known as the Kenites, a group of mostly nomadic clans whose main occupation was metalworking. The Kenites' more immediate Biblical ancestor was Jethro, the Medianite priest who befriended Moses and became his father-in-law when Moses married Zipporah. Jethro was also called "the Kenite," and his people were smiths. Because of Jethro's hospitality to Moses, the Kenites entered into a special relationship with the Jews. Centuries later, after King David also married a Kenite woman, most of the tribe was absorbed into the tribe of Judah. The Kenites continued their principal occupation as nomadic blacksmiths, but some settled down to farm around the holy Jewish city of Hebron in the Great Rift mountains on the west bank of the Jordan River. Others settled in the Negev Desert around Arad. The Israelites probably learned metalsmithing from their Kenite relatives, and not from the Philistines as some scholars have claimed.

King David's son, Solomon, founded the city of Etzion-Geber, near the present site of Eilat, as a center of copper and iron manufacturing. The metalworking was a

---

[6]Metallurgy is said by some to have started in northern Armenia, where the Ark of Noah supposedly survived atop Mt. Ararat, roughly ca. 3100 BCE.

highly profitable royal monopoly, and the metalworkers were Kenites and their Israelite apprentices. They helped to fuel the booming commerce between Israel and the ports of Ethiopia and Yemen.

In the centuries after Solomon and the subsequent schism that led to the Assyrian exile, some Kenite clans survived the successive invasions of the Holy Land by going south into Arabia. Or perhaps they traveled to Arabia from the northern outposts of Assyria, where the ten tribes disappeared. Forbes mentioned the wanderings of many Black Sea smiths through the Middle East. "The earliest signs of these ironsmiths are found with the nomads of the Syrian and Arabian desert, where they were the ancestors of the typical tinkers we find at the present time in Arabia."

He identifies these smiths as the despised and feared Kenite smiths of the desert. The Kenites "were mainly ironsmiths, who worshipped a thunder-and-fire god in Sinai," Forbes writes, noting the suggestion that the "sympathy between Hebrews and Kenites" stemmed from their common god.

The Hebrews and Kenites seemed to intermarry freely, Forbes said, and the Kenite progeny, including the Rechabites, were regarded by the Hebrew tribes as co-religionists and kin.

The Jewish nomads brought their metalworking trade to the oasis of Kheibar in Hejaz district, northwest of Medina, which had a sizable Jewish community long before Mohammed's time. Jews who settled in Kheibar after the destruction of the First Temple were said to have been ignorant of—or to have rejected—the growth of Talmudic law and later Jewish developments. Most Arabian Jews kept in close touch with Hebrew tradition and the evolving religion, but some groups remained outside this tradition. These Jews became like Ethiopia's Beta-Israel and the Bnei-Israel of India (as well as the Karaites, Samaritans and other Mosaic-based sects that either scorned or were cut off from the great changes in Judaism). S. D. Goiten, an expert in Arab-Jewish relations, says there is evidence that some Arabian Jews insisted on the written word of the Bible alone, rejecting entirely the later commentaries that became the Talmud, the Mishnah, and other rabbinical works.[7]

Before the seventh century and the advent of Mohammed, the only historical fact recorded about the Kheibar Jews was that al-Hareth al-A'raj, King Ghassan, attacked them in 524 CE—at the same time that their kinsman, Dhu-Nuwas, the Jewish king of Yemen, was at war with the Ethiopian invaders of southern Arabia. It is fair to surmise that these two Jewish populations of Arabia intermarried with each other in preference to their Christian and pagan Arab neighbors, thereby linking the Yemenite Jewish smiths to the Kenite Jews of Kheibar.

The Kheibar Jews were a formidable military force, successfully warding off attacks for centuries. But the smith clans were finally defeated by Mohammed's uncle, Omar, in 628 and most of the survivors were deported to Syria—in the tradition of deporting Jewish smiths that was followed

---

[7]Professor Moishe Perlman, however, insists that *all* of the Arabian Jews differed from the Falashas, who "are hardly just Ethiopian Jews . . . It is not only Talmudic lore they missed but Hebrew lore."

by Assyrians, Babylonians, Persians, Arabs and Ethiopians alike.

A few survivors managed to stay in Arabia and maintained their Judaic beliefs over the centuries, according to the medieval traveler Benjamin of Tudela and the 19th century Protestant missionary, Dr. Joseph Wolff. These claims are dismissed today, however, as total fabrications.

In the last century, the English traveler Doughty noted that the "foul soil" near Kheibar, which is "stained with rust," gave rise to the Arab fable that "this earth purges itself " of the Jewish blood spilt in the conquest of the oasis. It could have been blood mingled with the rust of metal shavings . . .

It is certain that some of the captured smiths of Yemen and perhaps of Kheibar were taken to Ethiopia as slaves during those turbulent years and that they were among those who rejected the Talmud and remained out of the Arabian Jewish mainstream that was "part and parcel of Near Eastern Jewry."

Cline, in his book on black African metallurgy, stated that East Africa did not develop its ironsmithing until this same period (roughly 600 CE), receiving its stimulus from Ethiopia, whose armies occupied southern Arabia. But no scholar has directly tied the Jewish nomad smiths of Arabia to the black Jewish smiths of Ethiopia. Forbes, in his massive study of ancient metallurgy, did mention the "Faladshas" in one sentence in his discussion of the Kenites: "The gradual evolution of the tinker to the state of a true nomad did not heighten the respect of the desert tribes for him; he remained despised as the smith of the Somali or Masai or the Jewish smiths of the Faladshas of Abyssinia."

Jews were a pariah people, and the smiths even more so. The Kenites of Kheibar, the Jewish smiths of Yemen and the Beta-Israel of Ethiopia eked out their living in a hated occupation, becoming virtual untouchables like the smiths of other tribes of northeast Africa.

THE FALASHA village smithy of the present day relies on scrap iron—mostly from the period of the Italian occupation—to perform his trade. Previously, the Falashas smelted metal from the iron ore that is so abundant in the highlands where they live.

The tribe's neighbors continue to disdain crafts and to rely on Falashas for iron tools and pottery. The Christian Ethiopian farmer fashions the wooden parts of his own plow, but he's likely to have purchased the metal parts from a Jewish smith.

One Beta-Israel blacksmith lives two miles outside the village of Ambover, in a hut off by itself at the edge of a steep descent. A deep gorge cuts through the rock below, creating an awesome chasm on three sides of the craftsman's *tekel*. Perhaps he and his family live in isolation because the aura of magic surrounding smithing affects the Falashas themselves, although Quirin suggests that ironworking "was highly valued within Beta-Israel society, as blacksmiths were considered to be respected and wise men." But it is significant that the only craft that Falasha priests are forbidden to practice is blacksmithing.

The smithy uses metal tongs and softens the iron over a charcoal fire while a helper works a goat-skin bellows to keep the fire hot. The Falasha smith uses a granite rock for his anvil, and swings a smoke-blackened hammer to shape the steel. Axes, adzes, knives and plow tips are fashioned, and ancient rifles are repaired: the smiths have devised molds and tools to recase every part of a rifle except the barrel.

Smithing is a skill that illuminates the story of the Beta-Israel. Perhaps, when a thorough study is undertaken, the survivors of the Kenite clans—from Israel, Kheibar, Syria and Yemen—may be linked to other "children of Moses," the Jewish smith tribe of Ethiopia.

Yemen's Jewish King

JUDAISM TRADITIONALLY does not seek converts. But there have been periods when Jewish evangelism rivaled the rapid spread of Christianity. Judaism was sweeping across the Middle East five hundred years before Jesus, and five hundred years after as well. There were Jewish colonies in Arabia and trade outposts in Nubia and Egypt which engaged in proselytizing. "The daughter of my dispersed is winning converts beyond the rivers of Ethiopia," according to Zephaniah. And the far-flung Jewish settlements were the source of the heavy Judaic influence in Ethiopia.

Two thousand years ago, during Roman control of the Red Sea region, Jewish coastal colonies in southern Arabia and Africa were flourishing; and the Roman geographer Strabo and others recorded the booming trade among Egypt, Ethiopia and India. The cities of South Arabia were described as gardens of the earth, rich in spices, flora and fauna—and Jews thrived in this paradise. Eventually, there

were even Jewish kings of South Arabia (the region was
called Saba, Sheba, Himyar and Yemen at various periods),
who emerged as Roman power declined. The trade wars of
these rulers may have inspired Abyssinian traditions of
Jewish Sea Kings— *bahr negast*. There was a sizable Jewish
population in southern Arabia when Rabbi Akiba traveled
there nineteen hundred years ago to arouse Diaspora support
against the Romans. The Yemenite Jews, according to their
tradition, had fled Israel forty-two years before the Romans
destroyed the Second Temple, in 70 CE. In writing of his
visit, the foremost of Israel's rabbis reported that the ruler of
southern Arabia was conspicuously different than the
Beduin Arabs. "He and his wife were quite black in color,
and he himself said that he was a *cushi* [Ethiopian]."

A few hundred years later, the ancient ties between
Israel, Ethiopia and South Arabia converged briefly in the
person of King Dhu-Nuwas, also known as Yosef or Asher,
who practiced a "particularly fanatical form" of Judaism
when he acceded to the throne of the independent Kingdom
of Himyar. Most scholars believe that this sixth century
ruler had a Jewish mother and was brought up as a Jew.

The anonymous Christian author of the sixth century
Book of the Himyarites related the story of Yemen's Jewish
monarch and the savage war between Christian Abyssinians
and the Arabian Jews. The writer did not try to conceal his
hatred for the Jewish king, whom he portrayed as
"murderer, crucifier and serpent; Satan incarnate." He ful-
minated against Dhu-Nuwas' origins: the son of a Jewish
woman, a slave who had been brought to Yemen from
Nisibis—an ancient Assyrian outpost on the Syrian-Turkish

border—where she had been purchased by the King of Yemen. The slave gave birth to Dhu-Nuwas, instructing him in Judaism and the traditions of her people. When his father died, Dhu-Nuwas became King of Himyar.

There were Jews throughout the Arabian peninsula at this time, when both Christianity and Judaism were spreading rapidly, and a military struggle in Arabia was inevitable. There were big power considerations as well, with Byzantium and Persia maneuvering for hegemony in the area. An Ethiopian army crossed the Red Sea and conquered the southern Arabian capital of Zafar in 517, and King Dhu-Nuwas marshaled his forces against the invaders.

According to the Christian version of events, Dhu-Nuwas first tried to win the Abyssinians to Judaism by sending "Jewish priests, who were from Tiberias" into Zafar. He also pledged peace and "swore oaths in the name of Adonai, and by the Ark, and the Torah." The Christian narrator claimed that Dhu-Nuwas then treacherously burned the church in Zafar with Ethiopians locked inside. He was called Satan by the Christians after he ordered newly converted Christians in his kingdom to "spit upon the cross and be Jews with us, and you shall live." If they refused his offer, the *Book of the Himyarites* alleged, he swore he would burn them "because you worship a mortal man who said he was the son of God." Some of those who resisted were tied to wild camels that dragged them into the desert.

Dhu-Nuwas marched against Najran in the north, after the Christians there killed a Jew named Daus Ben-Thalaban and then openly revolted against the Jewish monarch. He eventually retook the town, and most of the Ethiopian forces were withdrawn to Abyssinia. The Christian world may have greatly exaggerated the number of its dead in this opening round of war, but even today, some scholars, like Ullendorff, write that Dhu-Nuwas "engaged in an orgy of hatred, which led to the notorious massacre of Christians at Najran." The *Jewish Encyclopedia* takes the opposite tack, stating that the actual number of dead was relatively small, but that the events were blown out of proportion in order to serve as provocation for an international Christian campaign against the Jewish threat: Justinian I, the Byzantine emperor, wrote to his Ethiopian counterpart, Caleb—the Christian ruler nearest to South Arabia—and beseeched him to invade Himyar a second time, with a bigger force. In 525 an Ethiopian fleet, bolstered by Byzantine ships, crossed the narrow Red Sea straits dividing the two continents at Bab al-Mandeb, "The Gate of Tears."

The Persian rivals of Byzantium lined up with the Jews and pagan Arabs against Christian Arabs and Ethiopians. But Caleb had the upper hand when he returned to Arabia at the head of a huge army.

The Ethiopians clashed with King Dhu-Nuwas and his army in a bloody battle on the plain near the Red Sea, and crushed the Jewish forces. The "guilty king was killed and cut to pieces," bringing South Arabian independence to an end. The Christian account of the final battle said the Abyssinian soldiers who killed Dhu-Nuwas cut off the head of the despised "crucifier." The Ethiopians pursued the Jews "and destroyed them, just as reapers sweep the ears of the field." The Ethiopian soldiers proceeded through the towns of Yemen, slaughtering all those who did not have a cross tatooed on their hands. King Caleb was incredulous that some of the surviving Jews had dared to tatoo themselves in order to escape death or enslavement. "He wondered at their wickedness," according to the Christian narrative.

Another tradition relates this version of the Jewish king's demise: "When Dhu-Nuwas saw the fate that had befallen him and his people, he turned to the sea, and setting spurs to his horse . . . he plunged into the waves and nothing more of him was seen."

The death of the last Himyarite monarch stopped the spread of Judaism in Arabia, which was one of the main Christian intentions in the war. An equally important goal of the Christian world was to seize the strategic area of the Red Sea straits that controlled the trade route to India. Dhu-Nuwas was removed as an obstacle to the geopolitical and religious ambitions of Justinian and the Ethiopian ruler. For Dhu-Nuwas' zealous Judaism was not a freak occurrence—it was the result of an active Jewish political program devised by the Jews of Palestine and Arabia to counter the spread of Christianity.

In 1947, an inscription was discovered in the Ethiopian interior—in the region where the Beta-Israel are found—celebrating Caleb's victory over the Jewish king and Ethiopian hegemony over Yemen. It warned the Jewish proselytes in Ethiopia of similar consequences if they rose up against him. So it is conceivable that the Beta-Israel in Ethiopia not only knew of their coreligionists in Yemen, but also that they joined in the fighting against Caleb[1] in an international Christian-Jewish war.

The Jewish influence in Ethiopia must have been

---

[1]It is perhaps a curious coincidence that Caleb's son was named Beta Israel.

strengthened at this time by an influx of the enslaved Yemenite Jews. The captive Jews were led away from southern Arabia by the victorious Abyssinians, augmenting the Jewish community that already existed in Ethiopia.

[Today, the Falasha high priest claims that after Caleb's victory over the Jewish kingdom in Yemen, "There came yet another group of Jews to Ethiopia, led by Azonos and Phinhas . . . They became famous as missionaries and had a lot of success converting the pagan Agaw to Judaism."]

The Ethiopian occupation of South Arabia brought continuing persecution of the remaining Jewish population there. Abreha, Caleb's regent in Yemen, was advised by Bishop Grigentius to "take appropriate measures" to force the pagans and Jews to accept Christianity. But his efforts were cut short; and Abreha's successor was defeated by the Persians, who expelled the Ethiopian occupiers from Arabia.

The Jewish community existed in South Arabia throughout the next fourteen hundred years, until the 1950 Operation Magic Carpet, when about forty-three thousand Yemenite Jews were flown to the newly founded Jewish state from a British refugee camp in Aden.

The Yemenite Jews, like the Falashas, had the same racial characteristics as their neighbors, which had led observers to claim that "they are not Jews, but Judaized Arabs," just as the Beta-Israel are viewed as "Judaized Africans." The two remote Jewish communities in Yemen and in Ethiopia had strong ties established over the centuries. But unlike the Beta-Israel, the Yemenite Jews possessed the Talmud and read the holy books in Hebrew—a significant difference.

Illustrations

Two Beta-Israel elders who were Faitlovitch proteges (above), and a Falasha student in Europe during the 1930s

The sprawling provincial capital of Gondar

Schoolchildren in the large Falasha village of Ambover

By Louis Rapoport

A Beta-Israel religious leader (top left). A Falasha who came to Israel on her own (bottom). Schoolgirl in Ambover villege (top right). Jacques Faitlovitch (top right). Missionary Henry Stern preaching to the Falashas (right bottom).

By Gail Rubin

By Louis Rapoport

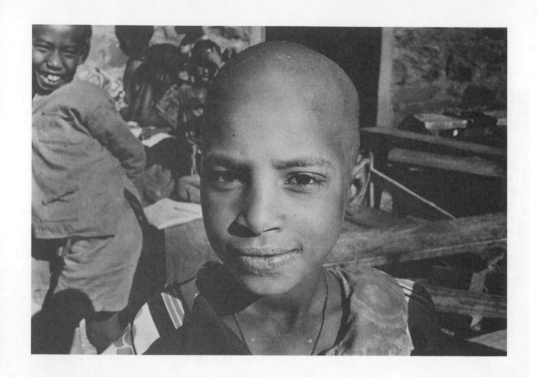

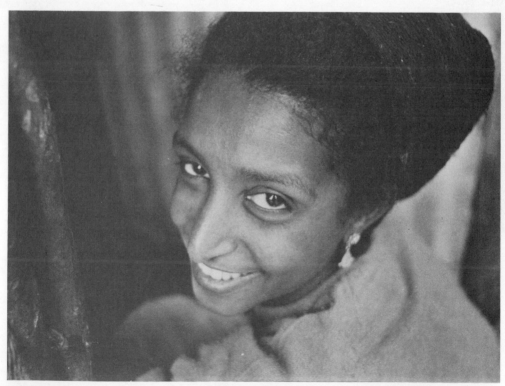

Photos by Louis Rapoport

A schoolboy in Saramlay village in the Gondar area (top left). The wife of a Beta-Israel religious teacher (bottom left). An Ethiopian painting (above) depicts Solomon's seduction of the Queen of Sheba

UGANDA WELCOMES YOU

Israeli Falashas played Ugandan soldiers in a movie about Entebbe

Falasha women, isolated during menstruation, pass the time doing handicrafts

Photos by Louis Rapoport

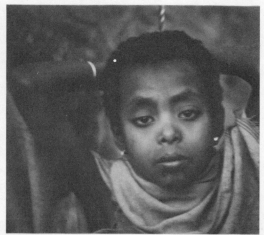

Photos by Louis Rapoport

Some faces of the 'Lost Tribe of Dan.' A Beta-Israel priest holds a Torah written in the Ge'ez language (top left). Next to him, a small girl dressed in sackcloth. Teachers in a Falasha primary school (bottom left). A girl wearing traditional robes (above right). Herdsmen with their cattle (above).

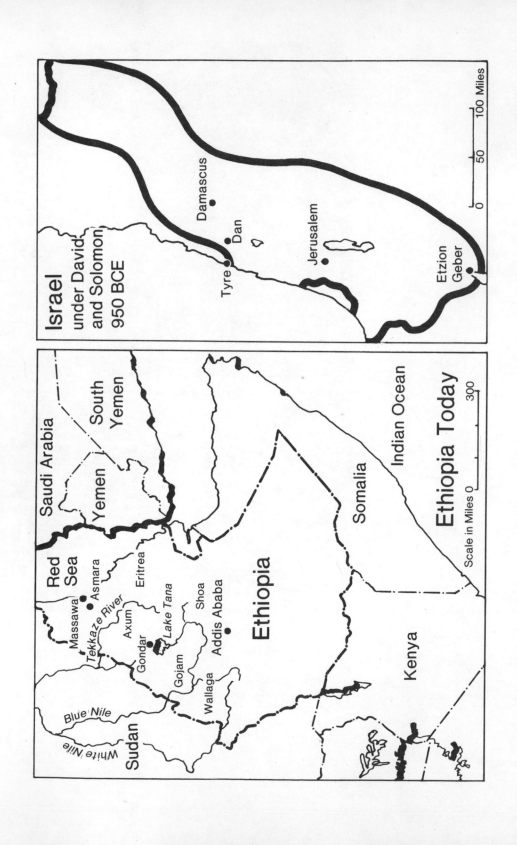

Israel under David and Solomon, 950 BCE

Damascus

Dan

Tyre

Jerusalem

Etzion Geber

0   50   100 Miles

Saudi Arabia

South Yemen

Yemen

Red Sea

Massawa

Asmara

Eritrea

Tekkaze River

Axum

Lake Tana

Shoa

Gondar

Addis Ababa

Gojam

Wallaga

Blue Nile

White Nile

Sudan

Ethiopia

Somalia

Indian Ocean

Kenya

Ethiopia Today

Scale in Miles 0   300

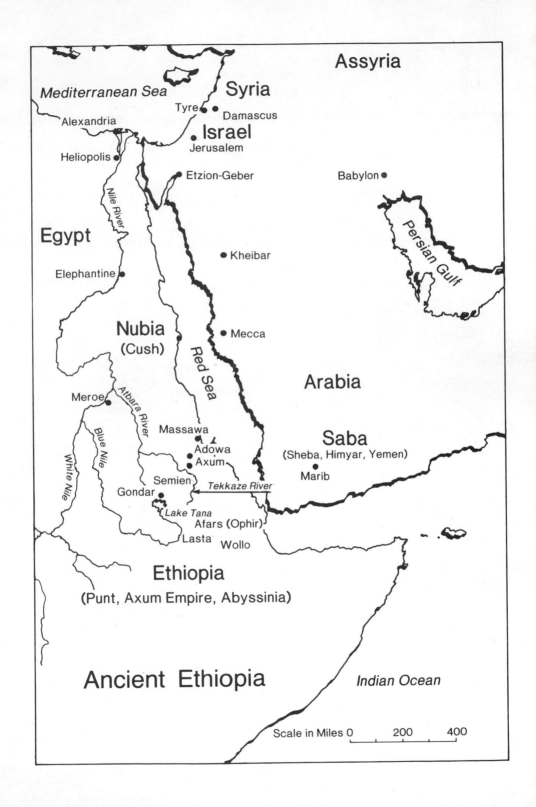

Assyria

Mediterranean Sea

Syria

Tyre • • Damascus

Alexandria

Israel

Jerusalem

Heliopolis •

Etzion-Geber

Babylon •

Persian Gulf

Egypt

Nile River

Elephantine •

Kheibar •

Nubia
(Cush)

Red Sea

Mecca •

Arabia

Meroe •

Atbara River

Massawa

Adowa
Axum •

Saba
(Sheba, Himyar, Yemen)

Marib •

Blue Nile

White Nile

Semien
Gondar •

Lake Tana

Tekkaze River

Afars (Ophir)

Lasta   Wollo

Ethiopia
(Punt, Axum Empire, Abyssinia)

Ancient Ethiopia

Indian Ocean

Scale in Miles 0   200   400

6

Secret of the Redemption

Falasha Queen

THERE ARE no Ethiopian texts extant that give the history of the Beta-Israel during the period before their greatest ruler, Queen Yehudit, reigned in the tenth century. All of the Falashas' written sources were destroyed during the four-hundred-year period of warfare against them that ended in the 17th century. And little is known about the rise of the Falasha kingdom before the tenth century, although it was referred to in the journals of travelers.

The Falashas had many kings called Gideon, and queens called Yehudit. In the Bible, Gideon was a warrior-judge, "raised up" by the Lord three thousand years ago as a "deliverer for the people of Israel." In a post-Biblical apocryphal work, Yehudit was a pious woman who saved the Jews by slaying an enemy general.

There are ample texts mentioning the reign of the powerful queen who devastated Christian Ethiopia around

135

975 CE. She was a Falasha woman of extraordinary beauty—
Yehudit. The Amhara, Ethiopia's long-dominant tribe, believe their language originated as a secret tongue during the
reign of the Jewish queen, whose rule marked a watershed in
Ethiopian history. Yet most Ethiopians today have never
even heard of Queen Yehudit's tribe, the Beta-Israel. The
country's historians, until recent years, barely mentioned
the Falashas, except to remark in passing that their rebel-
lions over the centuries had been suppressed. When the
Ethiopian writers did refer to Jews like Yehudit, it was
usually in the context that *all* Jews—black or white—were
the enemies of Christianity.

When Queen Yehudit vanquished the Christians, she
pulled down the monuments of ancient Axum, Africa's most
illustrious empire. There is scant written information regarding the origins of this "Falasha-Agaw" queen, although
stories about her abound in the oral histories of both Christians and Jews. One account explains her name: She was
called Yehudit[1] meaning "very beautiful," because no one
could be compared to her in beauty and finesse, except for
the Queen of Sheba.

But she was also called Gudit (evil) in Tigrean. Even
today, Ethiopian schoolchildren who have Falasha neighbors
make a play on the words "Yehudit the Gudit"—"evil
Jewess." She was called Gudit after she burned down the
Axum cathedral, the holiest site in the Abyssinian Christian

---

[1]Yehudit is the Hebrew for Judith, and *yahoudya* means Jewess. In Ge'ez, Yehudit
means beautiful. The queen was also called Ester and Esato. The various names
applied to the queen have led scholars to different conclusions about her origins.

domain. Yehudit was said to be descended from the royal Jewish family, the daughter of Gideon and Yehudit, rulers of the independent Beta-Israel kingdom in Semien. Yehudit's mother country has also been identified as being near Adowa in Tigre, close to Ethiopia's "Second Jerusalem" of Axum, the capital city she would eventually capture and destroy.

The fallen monuments of Axum show inscriptions left by the people of Saba, the empire that included Ethiopia and South Arabia and that was called Sheba in the Bible. Axum was the African capital of this bicontinental empire. Its founder was Menelik, son of the Queen of Sheba and the king of Israel, whose Semitic-Cushitic dynasty ruled an area that became a crossroads of the ancient world—the stelae at Axum date from before the fourth century BCE. It was an enduring empire, influenced by Egypt, Greece, Syria and Israel. When it turned Christian in the fourth century, the city of Axum was transformed from "Jerusalem" to "Rome."

To the Ethiopian tribes that resisted Christianity over the next millenium, Axum represented the essence of evil. The Agaw in general, and the Beta-Israel in particular, fought fiercely over the centuries with the goal of destroying Axum. There is no question that the Falashas' strong allegiance to Judaism was the sustaining factor in their struggle and their greatest leader in the warfare that spanned at least twelve hundred years was Yehudit, the warrior queen.

According to one legend, the young Yehudit had spent several years in Syria—where there were large Jewish colonies—before she returned to Ethiopia with a male companion, Zenobis. She soon gathered a large following and sent messages to her home country around Adowa: "Come to me immediately and join me. Anyone who doesn't come will share the same fate as my enemy." As she made her way from Eritrea, the people from surrounding villages flocked around her. In the course of a few weeks, she managed to assemble a formidable army.

A Ge'ez text relates that Yehudit carved out a new route from the Red Sea port of Massawa, taking her enemies by surprise. No force could stop her or slow her down, and she entered Axum after overcoming only feeble resistance. An Ethiopian text relates: "First she destroyed the palace and then the cathedral that was built by Abreha and Asbeha of gold, silver and diamonds down to the foundations. The stelae which were constructed by Greek craftsmen and cost so much money were overthrown and broken by hammers. The wells of water were blocked so that people could not draw from them and the country became a desert, as if it had never been inhabited."

Then she issued a decree: "Churches should be closed because I am a Jew and my husband is also a Jew."

Another version says that Yehudit married the Lord of Begwena in the Agaw district of Lasta and "intensified the persecution of the Ethiopian priests and the people." She ruled northern Ethiopia for forty years, the Christian account says.

During her reign, the Ark of the Covenant, which the Christians had removed from Axum just before she captured the city, was kept in a safe region to the south: "Sion, the Ark of the Tabernacle of the Law, never fell into her hands." The Ethiopian tradition is that the Ark was removed to

Debra Seyon monastery, "and watched vigilantly for forty years," until Yehudit's death.

It should be noted that the Ethiopian accounts of Yehudit were set down centuries after her reign, and they are tinged with the contempt reserved for implacable enemies of Christianity. This was also true of the main contemporary account of Jewish King Dhu-Nuwas in his battles against the Ethiopian invaders of South Arabia—it is a Christian version of events.

There is a bizarre twist to Queen Yehudit's story in this Abyssinian legend: As a young woman, she came to Axum and became a prostitute. She rebuffed one eager youth who asked to spend the night with her, saying, "You are from the priestly caste and I am from the royal family. How dare you try to sleep with me?" He asked what he could do to persuade her to change her mind, and she said, "First of all bring this present—a gold veil and golden shoes. Only then will you succeed." The young man, who had fallen in love with Yehudit, vowed he would do anything to get the gifts. He went to Axum's Treasury of Zion—*seyon*, the Ark, where the Holy Tabernacle was kept—and tore out a piece of gold curtain big enough to cover the feet of his beloved.

When the people of Axum found that "Gudit's" shoes were fashioned from this stolen, holy gold, they assembled to pass judgement. Their verdict: "What can a boy of twenty do when he sees such beauty. He is innocent. She is the only one responsible for the desecration of the curtain of Zion." They passed sentence on Yehudit: Her right breast was cut from her body, and she was ordered into exile. "And they chased her to the Red Sea, which was the boundary of

Egypt . . ." This tale of the Ark's golden curtain can be compared with the *Kebra Negast* story that the Queen of Sheba had asked Solomon to send her the gold curtain so it could be worshipped in her country. It is one of several significant parallels between the two queens.

Yehudit, the mutilated "whore of Axum," traveled along the Mediterranean shore through Palestine, according to this account. Zenobis, the son of the king of Sham (Syria), found Yehudit on the beach and asked her where she had come from and what had happened to her. She showed him her ravaged breast, and "he was shocked, and he sympathized with her." Zenobis fell in love with the beautiful princess and married her. The Christian version says that she embraced Judaism because her husband was a Jew. She became fanatical in her beliefs and determined to bring Judaism back to Ethiopia, where it had once thrived. It was then that she persuaded Zenobis to leave Syria[2] and help her gather an army to conquer Abyssinia.

There is other mention of Yehudit in historical sources: Sawrius' *History of the Patriarchs of Alexandria* refers to a pagan queen of the "Bani al-Hamwiyah" who led her people against the Christians in the tenth century. A medieval Moslem traveler and scholar, Ibn Hankal, described the Ethiopian queen who had defeated and killed the king of Abyssinia and who ruled a vast empire from "the regions of the land of the *hadani* in the west of Abyssinia." (The word

---

[2] Most Jews of tenth century Syria were metalsmiths or merchants; in 969, the first vizier was a Jewish convert to Islam who remained loyal to the Jews. Other Jews were among the leading officials.

hadani—"the Danite" in Hebrew—may have been the name of the Beta-Israel before the term *falasha* came into use.)

Queen Yehudit left a grim landmark behind her: In Gondar Province today, in the area where the Agaw and Beta-Israel live, there are two heaps of stones side by side— one very large, the other considerably smaller. The local people attribute these rock piles to the Jewish queen. Each of her soldiers deposited a stone on the way to and from a major battle with the Oromo, who had conquered southern Ethiopia. The queen measured the difference in the two heaps to assess her losses, which apparently were very great. The stones were piled on a mountain called Gobedra— archeologists have found an engraved lioness on this spot— along an ancient caravan route between Ethiopia's gold mines and Axum. The route from the capital crossed the Tekkaze River and proceeded to the southwest. It is not surprising that this highway to gold country was a vital military target for the Falasha monarch, as it must have been for the Queen of Sheba two thousand years earlier.

Queen Yehudit had threatened the foundations of Christianity in Ethiopia. She had even massacred the royal Abyssinian family—who were regarded as demigods—at Debra Damo, a difficult-to-reach place that was formerly the royal prison. "The lands are abandoned without a shepherd and our bishops and priests are dead, and the churches are ruined," the Amhara successor king wrote to the monarch of neighboring Nubia.

After Yehudit's death, the Ethiopian rulers rebuilt the cathedral of Axum and ordered churches built throughout the area, where "the Christian faith had been shaken by the attempted persecution by Gudit." The Beta-Israel's neighbors never forgave them for this.

A Beta-Israel version of the Jewish queen's origins was recorded in 1973. The Falasha high priest said that Queen Yehudit was a daughter of Gideon IV, who rebelled against the Amharas when they tried to convert the Falashas to Christianity. "This was the reason that she burnt churches and killed Christian priests. But she was defeated when Moslem tribes from Eritrea joined the Christian forces, who took revenge on the Falashas for many years," the priest said.

Until today, the Beta-Israel have suffered because of beliefs related to the legends of Queen Yehudit's anti-Christian campaign. This curse has been especially prevalent in the sub-province of Lasta, in Wollo. The curse was on the lips of a hired band of murderers in 1972 when they entered a Falasha village there and killed twenty-nine persons.

The Hill of the Jews

THE JEWISH TRIBE lived in relative security for three hundred years after the climactic reign of Yehudit, who had temporarily ended the rule of the Amhara dynasty that traced its ancestry to Solomon and Sheba. It was replaced by an Agaw dynasty called the Zagwe, who, like the Amhara, were also Christians, although the Zagwe claimed descent from Moses as well as from Solomon. The Beta-Israel prospered under the Zagwe, perhaps because they may have shared the same Agaw ethnic background.

The Zagwe kings welcomed Jewish immigrants from Yemen during this period of toleration, according to an Ethiopian manuscript. A family of Jewish traders from Aden, led by Joseph, who was "exceedingly rich and wealthy," settled in Ilawz "in the land of Amhara," and prospered there.

Another Ethiopian chronicle, which may refute the theory that the Beta-Israel were Agaw kinsmen of the Zagwe dynasty, says: "Now it came to pass that the kingdom passed to *another*[3] people [after Yehudit and the Falashas] who were *not* of the tribe of Israel; these people were called the Zagwe . . ."

The toleration extended to the Beta-Israel ended in the 13th century, when the Zagwe were overthrown and the Amhara Solomonic line was restored. These Abyssinian emperors, expanding their territory as they conducted a Christian crusade, set out to destroy the Ethiopian Jews. In 1270 Emperor Yekuno Amlak vowed to end Beta-Israel independence; he said that the Jews could not be relied upon in the struggle against Moslem kingdoms, which were threatening to overrun Ethiopia. Amlak's declaration was the beginning of four hundred years of religious war.

In the early 14th century, when both the Amhara and the Moslems were enlarging their holdings in northwest Ethiopia, the Beta-Israel tipped the balance of power. At first, the Jewish ruler, Gideon, joined the Moslems in their battles against Amda Seyon ("Pillar of Zion"), the Amhara warrior king who ruled from 1314 to 1344. But when the

---

[3] My italics.

Moslems pillaged the area around Gondar, including
Falasha villages, the Beta-Israel switched sides. The
Moslems captured Gideon and his queen but resistance continued, and the Christians and their Jewish allies managed
to push back the Moslem incursion.

The Falashas had only a short respite, however, before
the Amhara resumed their war against them. Amda Seyon
sent his forces with the command to "devastate the Falashas
and subject them to the rule of Christ."

News of these medieval religious wars reached the
Cabbalists of Safad in northern Palestine, and they are mentioned in Abraham Halevi's *Letter on the Secret of the Redemption*.

The famous Scottish explorer of the Blue Nile, James
Bruce, was deeply moved when he encountered several
Ethiopian Jews in Gondar in 1770. His travel memoirs,
which are an invaluable source for students of Ethiopia, also
provided the first solid information about Beta-Israel history
from the 13th to the 17th century, the period in which their
shrunken kingdom was almost constantly threatened.

According to Bruce, even after the fall of the last
Falasha king the Beta-Israel fought under other rulers to
maintain a measure of independence, sometimes offering
their support to enemies of the Amhara emperors. During
the reign of Emperor Dawit I (1382-1411), warfare against
the Falashas intensified. An apostate Amhara monk called
Qozimos converted to the Beta-Israel religion and took
refuge among them. Qozimos, who claimed that he was the
messiah, incited the Beta-Israel to battle the Christians of
Dembia and of the monasteries east of Lake Tana. It was

probably Qozimos who introduced monasticism to the Beta-Israel, an un-Jewish custom that was preserved until recent years.

Dawit's successor, Yeshaq (1413-1430), was very adept at exploiting divisions among the Beta-Israel, playing one chieftain against another. The tribe no longer had a king, and was only semi-autonomous by this period. Yeshaq appointed a Falasha leader, Bet-Ajir, as governor of Semien and Dembia and installed the chieftain's nephew as a watchdog and liaison to the imperial court. When Bet-Ajir refused to continue to be a tribute-paying vassal, Yeshaq led an army against him. "They made war from morning to evening. After that, Bet-Ajir escaped; but the soldiers of the king surrounded him and cut off his head," according to an Amhara manuscript. Falasha leaders who collaborated with Yeshaq were rewarded.

Ethiopian historian Taddesse Tamrat, suggests that Yeshaq was fully aware of the "essentially religious nature of the Falasha question." The only way to end this recurring problem was by imposing Christianity on the "rebeling infidels." This is when he passed the fateful decree taking away forever the tribe's right to own land.

The Jews once again gave refuge to Christian rebels during the reign of Zar'a Yaqob ("Seed of Jacob"), Yeshaq's successor. The rebels included one of the emperor's sons, who converted to Judaism and found refuge with a Falasha monk called Abba Sabra. Several regional rulers also converted to Judaism at this time. Zar'a Yaqob ordered all pagans and Jews in his realm either to become Christians or die, for the Beta-Israel had become a major religious threat, whose Judaism was attracting increasing numbers of Christians. When Zar'a Yaqob died, Baeda Mariam (1468–1478) carried on the campaign. His expedition against the Falashas was made possible by a temporary truce with the Moslem states, and Baeda Mariam killed an enormous number of Falashas in Semien and Sakalt.

A generation later, a new element entered Abyssinia— the Portuguese, who introduced firearms into Ethiopia during their expeditions in the late 15th and early 16th centuries.

The Ethiopian Jews, as long as they had semi-autonomy and a fighting force, could and did switch their allegiance between the warring Moslems and Christians—it was necessary to survive. In 1541, when a four-hundred-man Portuguese expedition arrived in Abyssinia, a Somali Moslem leader—Iman Ahmed, known as Gran—was threatening to conquer the whole country. The Beta-Israel were once again drawn into conflict.

The Portuguese force, under Dom Christovao de Gama, eventually killed Gran and drove the invading Somalis out of Ethiopia, and the Beta-Israel played a pivotal role in this success. "A Jew came to Christovao," according to the records of the expedition, and told the Portuguese of a mountain stronghold that he had commanded until it fell to the Moslems. "The Jew said ten thousand to twelve thousand of his people inhabited the Hill of the Jews" and offered to guide the Portuguese there by way of an "unsuspected access." The Falasha promised the Europeans booty—one hundred and fifteen strong horses—and they agreed to the plan. The Portuguese made rafts of animal skins for the crossing of the Tekkaze River and then set out

for the strategic fortress in the fifteen thousand-foot-high
Semien mountains.

The force took the Moslems by surprise, as the Falasha
had pledged. The Somalis who escaped the Portuguese "fell
at the hands of the Jew inhabitants, who followed in pursuit
of the Moor." The Jews "blocked the passes in the hills,
with which they were well-acquainted and killed nearly all,
including the captain, and captured all the spoils they could
carry and their women."

The Falashas brought everything to Christovao, including the Moslem captain's head and his very beautiful
wife, whom Christovao took for himself.

According to this Jesuit chronicle, "the Jew inhabitants, astonished at the [Portuguese] feat of arms, became
Christians . . . The Jew captain asked to be baptized and
when we got to the hill and pitched our camp, I baptized
him, his wife and his son."

IT HAS BEEN noted that the steepest places were at all
times the asylum of liberty, terrain easy to defend. The
towering Semien range, whose isolation also fostered superstition about its inhabitants, provided the last military
stronghold for the Beta-Israel in their struggle against
Moslem invaders and Christian warrior kings.

In 1559 the Beta-Israel, under a new leader, Redai,
rose up once again, repulsing the forces of the Amhara
rulers—Claudius and later, Minas—and actually expanding
Falasha holdings in the area of the Hill of the Jews. Redai
had angered the Abyssinians by renaming the mountains of
Semien after those of the Torah—Sinai and Tabor.

Minas and his successor, Sarsa Dengel (1563-1597)

campaigned against the Jews during the next four years. It was tortuous terrain, with roads hanging above steep gorges, and many transport animals fell into the chasms below. According to historian Robert Hess, "The Ethiopians were not prepared for the excessive cold of the higher mountains of Woggera and Semien. Moreover, the Falashas deliberately destroyed the paths so that they could not be used by mules and horses, and from their heights, they rolled boulders down upon their attackers.

"Lastly, Kaleb, Redai's brother and commander of one group of Falashas, pursued a scorched earth policy that hindered the movements of the Amhara army, which usually lived off the land. But the Ethiopians had a decisive advantage from the start. Unlike the Falasha, who fought with lance and shield the Amhara were now equipped with guns."

The Portuguese-supplied arms made all the difference in this campaign, which was much bloodier than previous ones.

"When Sarsa Dengel ordered cannon to be brought up, the fate of the Falasha was sealed," Dr. Joseph Halevy wrote in *Guerre de Sarsa Dengel*.

Beta-Israel men and women fought to the death from the steep heights of their fortress. They threw themselves over the precipice or cut each other's throats rather than be taken prisoner—it was a Falasha Masada. Twenty-two years after the last major Falasha uprising had begun, Redai surrendered the stronghold and was taken away in chains.

This decisive battle was fought at a place called Mashaka, near the Marek River, identified by some as the

Hill of the Jews. Sarsa Dengel celebrated his great victory with a Mass on top of Redai's mountain in which all of the Falashas' histories and all of their religious books were burned, some of them probably in Hebrew—it was an attempt to eradicate forever the Judaic memory of Ethiopia.

Two centuries after the battle, explorer James Bruce would pass a place called Hill of the Jews, or Jews' Rock (*ambda ayhud* in Amharic). He wrote, inaccurately, that the mountain stronghold was "still possessed by Jews . . . And there Gideon and Judith, king and queen of that nation, and, as they say, of the House of Judah, maintain still their ancient sovereignty and religion from very early times."

But the exact location of Jews' Rock, somewhere in the mountain fastnesses of Semien, remains unknown.

Sarsa Dengel, who traded in slaves to finance his many wars, dispersed the defeated Beta-Israel whom he didn't sell. He settled two hundred of the Jews at Amba-Warq—"gold mountain," for the Jews were always associated with gold in the minds of the superstitious.

There was an Ethiopian tradition that the Falashas had much gold, and when Redai surrendered, the Christians were furious that no treasure was found. This legend of the Jews' buried gold in the mountains of Woggera or Semien has persisted to the present day. After defeating Redai, Sarsa Dengel took a Jewish woman from Semien as his concubine. She has been identified by one scholar as Harago, who may have been Redai's sister. When the Ethiopian emperor died in 1597 there was a succession struggle among his three sons, all of whom had a Jewish mother.

Sarsa Dengel broke the back of Jewish resistance, but

sporadic fighting continued for another thirty-five years before the Falashas were totally subjugated. The last vestige of Beta-Israel independence ended during the reign of Susneyos, 1607-1632. The Falashas once again had given refuge to rival pretenders to the Amhara throne—some of whom were considered to be their Jewish kinsmen. In revenge, Susneyos in 1616 ordered the extermination of all Jews from Lake Tana to the Semien mountains. The Falashas' children were taken from them and sold into slavery, James Bruce wrote. Amdo, a Jewish leader, was crucified. The surviving Ethiopian Jews became an impoverished, downtrodden people.

According to a 19th-century Falasha manuscript, an "Israelite" named Abraham became the chief counselor to Susneyos after the Beta-Israel had been broken, "and the king loved him." He granted Abraham a wish, and Abraham asked that the Falashas be allowed to return to the Jewish belief that Susneyos had forced them to renounce. "I give you all the Israelites who are in my territory," the ruler said. This occurred at the end of Susneyos' reign, when he granted a small measure of religious freedom throughout his realm. Despite his earlier edict to exterminate the Falashas in two provinces, Susneyos apparently killed fewer Jews than did his predecessor, Sarsa Dengel.

In the later part of the 17th century, under Emperor Fasiledes, the Beta-Israel enjoyed a measure of prosperity even though their status had been permanently lowered. Fasiledes used special squadrons of Falasha soldiers in his bodyguard, and Jewish craftsmen were employed to build his castles in Gondar, which he founded and declared Ethiopia's capital.

The Falashas, who had turned to their monks for guidance after the defeat of their last political leaders, were forbidden in perpetuity from owning land—Yeshaq had issued the first, most significant decree: "He who is baptized in the Christian religion may inherit the land of his father; otherwise, let him be a *falasi*." And the emperors that followed elaborated on the edict. There were a few exceptions to the ban—for example, when gifts were bestowed on favored Jewish craftsmen. But for the most part the Beta-Israel were kept landless until the overthrow of Haile Selassie in 1974.

Over the centuries, the Amhara deported thousands of Falasha metalworkers, weavers, masons and potters from their mountain homes in Semien and Woggera to Shoa, Wallo, Tigre, Lasta and Gojjam, where many became Christians—including the *tabiban*, the Marranos of Ethiopia.

During and after what is known as Ethiopia's Period of the Wars, 1270-1632, there were massive executions of Falashas and tens of thousands of others were sold into slavery, until the tribe's numbers were reduced from more than a million to two hundred thousand in the 19th century.

There were no more major battles in the two-hundred-year Gondar Era that followed the Period of the Wars, but the Beta-Israel were locked in struggle against efforts to enslave, convert and enfeeble them further. The Falashas were considered to be prime merchandise during the booming days of the slave trade, in the 18th and 19th centuries. Arthur Rimbaud, the French poet who spent his waning years in Abyssinia during the 1880's, was a slave dealer in the trade center of Harar. His wife may have been a Tigrean

Falasha. Slaves are still being sold in Ethiopia; and slave import in neighboring Arabia was not officially banned until 1962. The Beta-Israel, like the Kemant tribe, lived along a major slave route. And the Jews of Ethiopia were in great demand among Arab slave owners.

OVER THE CENTURIES, between episodes of war and oppression, there were periods of tranquility for the Beta-Israel, when their creative life was allowed to flourish; it was not a history of unceasing torment. But after 1755 and the eclipse of imperial power, their building skills were no longer in demand and the tribe's fortunes sank lower, until its members became virtual untouchables.

They reached a pitiful nadir in their history in 1862. In an evangelistic reaction against an invasion by English Protestant missionaries who were backed by the emperor, the Beta-Israel tried to leave Ethiopia en masse. As noted earlier, a false messiah arose among them, a monk from Dembia named Abba Mahari, who claimed he had had a vision and would lead his people to Jerusalem. He promised that the Bible miracles would occur again, that the Red Sea would part for the Jews. They crossed the Tekkaze River and circled the Christian holy city of Axum, whose cathedral was said to hold the Ark of Zion. They believed that God would help them, that they didn't need arms to conquer Axum, which would fall as Jericho had. They believed that the Christians would be forced to return the Ark of the Covenant to the Jews, and then the Falashas would take it back to the Land of Israel. "To their dismay, they received nothing but blows and insults. Many died of hunger and malaria," a missionary wrote. The survivors settled in the southern part of Tigre province, north of the Tekkaze River.

In the years that followed, the diminished tribe again resisted foreign invaders: In the 1880s, when they sided with the Christians against the Mahdi of Sudan and his Moslem Dervishes, and in the 1930s, when the Beta-Israel fought tenaciously against the Italian fascist invaders. The Italians wiped out entire Falasha villages in reprisal for a guerrilla attack, and the Ethiopian Jews were singled out for harsh treatment throughout the six-year occupation. During the Italian war, in an attempt to retain their tribal identity, many Beta-Israel resettled in remote regions.

Jewish Travelers

THE FIRST mention of a Jewish community in Ethiopia was made eleven hundred years ago. Eldad Hadani (the Danite), the ninth-century Jewish traveler who claimed that he belonged to the lost tribe of Dan, wrote in his diaries that his tribe and three other tribes of Israel had survived in a mountainous area of northeast Africa, a region akin to the Semien range in Ethiopia, the Beta-Israel's ancient strong-hold.

The tribes of Dan, Naphtali, Gad and Asher left Assyria after the death of Sennacherib in 681 BCE and journeyed to the "land of gold"—Ethiopia—Eldad reported. In Africa, they were constantly at war with their neighbors: "And they slew the men of Ethiopia, and unto this very day, they fight with the children of the kingdoms of Ethiopia." Eldad said that the sons of Samson—the Danites—were superior to all in battle. The Israelite tribes, who had come to Ethiopia after spending some time in Egypt, were mostly nomadic people; but a large number of Jews settled near the mythical Sambatyon River. It was possible to "see and talk to the sons of Moses," but not to cross the river, Eldad said.

The Sambatyon is a key element in the mystery surrounding the Falashas' origins. Find the Sambatyon and you will find the lost tribes of Israel, according to legend. The river has been placed in America, China, Syria and many other countries. Eldad's contemporaries said the river was in the land of Prester John, the legendary ruler of a Christian empire that was identified with Ethiopia. The Prophet Isaiah described Ethiopia as the land "cut by the rivers." There are no navigable rivers in the highlands of the Great Rift, where the waters rush along gorges and mile-deep ravines, creating an impassable barrier to travelers.

According to one Beta-Israel legend recorded in the 19th century, Menelik, the son of Solomon and Sheba's queen, on his return to Ethiopia from Jerusalem crossed a river on the Sabbath with the Holy Ark of the Covenant, which he had stolen from the Temple. Those of his company who crossed over with him became Christians. Those who refused—thereby observing the Sabbath—were the progenitors of the Ethiopian Jews.

There is a river that fits the general descriptions of Genesis, Isaiah, Eldad and the Falashas, and in part those of Josephus, Pliny and Rabbi Akiba as well. It is the Tekkaze River, the ancient boundary of the Ethiopian Jews, where legend said Moses had destroyed an Ethiopian dam built to choke off the Nile headwaters. The Tekkaze, worshipped as a god by the pagan Agaw, is a tributary of the Atbara River, separating Gondar and Semien from Tigre. In its rapid descent from the highlands, it cuts fiercely through ever-deepening chasms. Its whirlpools add to the extreme hazards of crossing this torrent, which is fed by hundreds of swift tributaries as it courses its way into the Blue Nile—identified as the River Gihon of Genesis, the main artery of Cush. Masses of cane and mimosa bushes overhang the churning Tekkaze. "And the sons of Moses could not cross it," Eldad said. The towering Semien mountains rise out of the deep ravines and rest in the huge bend that the river weaves. The dramatic topography of the Great Rift is nowhere more evident than here, where the earth seems to have been cleaved by a giant hand.

Eldad said that the river was full of sand and stones, which "make a great noise like the waves of the sea and a stormy wind, so that in the night the noise is heard at a distance of half a day's journey . . . and this river of stone and sand rolls during the six working days and rests on the Sabbath day, when fire surrounds the river." Although the rolling waters of the Sambatyon came to a stop, it was still impassable for the Jewish tribes, who were not allowed to cross a river on the Sabbath. The Beta-Israel to this day will not cross a river on the day of rest.

The Midrash says that "The Ten Tribes wandered into exile on the other side of the River Sambatyon," and lost all connection with their Jewish brethren. They were cut off from the major developments in Judaism—the Talmud and rabbinical tradition. The "Sons of Moses know not the rabbis, for these were of the Second Temple and they did not reach them," Eldad wrote. He reported that "They do not read the Roll of Esther, not having been included in the miraculous salvation mentioned in it."

Scholars make divergent guesses regarding Eldad Hadani's origins. He was a South Arabian, or a Falasha, or a Karaite. Some say he was an imposter. S. D. Goitein wrote that "He was neither merely a literary romancer nor a disguised Karaite, but simply a Falasha of Abyssinia." Eldad's *halachic* (Jewish law) writings were quoted by outstanding medieval commentators, including the great Rashi.

Scholars who are skeptical of Eldad's accounts say that they are only embellishments based on real Jewish rulers and kingdoms: Dhu-Nuwas of Yemen, the Beta-Israel kingdom in northwest Abyssinia, and the Khazari of eastern Europe. Ethiopia expert Edward Ullendorff claims that Eldad "shows no firsthand knowledge of Abyssinia." But others contend that he undoubtedly traveled in northeast Africa. And the geographical references he provided concerning the lost tribe of Dan would become extremely important in the slow awakening of world Jewry to the existence of this black Jewish tribe in the remote Ethiopian mountains. He placed the lost tribes in Cush, and this report would be cited a millenium later, when Israel's chief Sephardic rabbi quoted Eldad as a basic authority for recognizing the Falashas as Jews.

THREE CENTURIES after Eldad's death, Benjamin of Tudela, the Jewish merchant-traveler from Spain, mentioned the Ethiopians in describing the descendants of the ten lost tribes. After a journey between Yemen and Egypt, Benjamin recounted his visits to the towns and fortresses of

the Jews of South Arabia and northeast Africa. "There are
Jews who are not subject to the rule of others, and they have
towns and fortresses on the tops of mountains," he wrote.
He also claimed to have encountered lost tribes in Persia—
he placed the Danites in Nishapur—and in the Kheibar
Oasis of Arabia.

In 1438 an Italian Jew, Elijah of Ferrara, wrote of his
meeting in Jerusalem with a young Ethiopian Jew, who told
him of long and successful wars fought by Jews in the
mountains of Ethiopia. Elijah was told that the Falashas had
a language of their own, "neither Hebrew nor Ishmaelite."

Obadiah of Bertinoro, in his letters from Jerusalem,
also mentioned the Ethiopian Jews. He reported seeing
some Falashas in Egypt, and revived the story that the lost
tribes were at war with the legendary Christian monarch,
Prester John. Obadiah, writing in 1489, also said that the
Sambatyon River could be found at a distance of fifty days'
journey from Aden (Yemen), where it separated the terri-
tories of the Children of Moses from other tribes.

Later in the 15th century, the great Radbaz, Rabbi
David Ben Zimra, passed his judgment in Cairo on the
validity of marriage between an Egyptian Jew and a Falasha
woman. In his opinion, the Beta-Israel were basically Jews
with strange customs. This was a landmark decision for the
Beta-Israel.

By the 16th century, there were increasing references
to the Ethiopian Jews. Isaac Akrish reported from Con-
stantinople of a "Jewish-Ethiopian Prince who had allied
himself with Moslems against Christians." Moses de Rossi
and Abraham Yagel wrote of Jews in the Mountains of the

Moon—Uganda. And the word "Falashas" appeared in the writings of the Cabbalists of Safed, when Abraham Halevi identified them with the lost tribes.

DAVID REUVENI, the Jewish adventurer who raised messianic hopes in the early 16th century, was—like Eldad Hadani—probably a Falasha. He claimed to be the son of a king who had ruled the lost tribes of Reuben (hence his name), Gad and the half-tribe of Manasseh in the desert of Habor—Mesopotamia. But in his diaries and letters, he also claimed direct descent from King David and the tribe of Judah. Reuveni was said to have been redeemed by the Jews of Alexandria from Arab slave traders. He then traveled to Jerusalem, claiming that he had been sent on his mission by the "King of the Lost Tribes" to hasten the Redemption. He spread messianic hopes along his way, in Safed, Damascus, Venice and in Rome, where he was received by Pope Clement VII. Reuveni asked the pope for a letter to "King Prester John" of Ethiopia and to European monarchs, recommending that they give arms to Reuveni so that his "state" could join the Christian world in the war against the Moslems. In 1525 Reuveni received a royal reception from the Portuguese king. During this stay in Lisbon he made significant headway in winning support among the Marranos. But he was eventually expelled by the Inquisition authorities, and taken to Spain in chains, charged with seducing New Christians to return to Judaism. Reuveni perished in prison but he left behind a long account of the lost tribes with a companion, Abraham Farissol.

During the 16th century, Portuguese Jesuits brought

news of the Falashas to Europe. But direct contact between Western Jews and the Beta-Israel was not made until the 19th century, at the height of the Christian missionary campaign to convert the surviving Jews of Ethiopia.

7

Struggle for Souls

Stern at the Stake

"The unexpected breath of heaven now agitating the dry bones of Israel on the mountain-tops of Africa, seems an unmistakable indication that our work enjoys the Divine favor."

      . . . Protestant missionary Henry Stern

THE FALASHAS were rediscovered by world Jewry in the 19th century when it seemed certain that Protestant missionaries from England would convert the Ethiopian Jews, and that the tribe would assimilate and disappear. The Jewish-Christian struggle over the Beta-Israel was to have a profound effect on the tribe's fate.

The nature of the religious struggle has prejudiced research on the Beta-Israel by "interested parties" from both sides. As Wolf Leslau noted in his *Falasha Anthology*: "Most of the reports that have so far been made about the Falashas are incomplete and characterized by a Christian or Jewish missionary tendency which appreciably diminishes their value."

Jesuits preceded the Protestants to Ethiopia by three hundred years, accompanying Portuguese soldiers into the country in 1541. The Jesuits charged that there was a "dangerous Hebraic mould" to the Abyssinian Christian church, which was founded in the fourth century when a shipwrecked Syrian Christian converted the Ethiopian ruler. The Jesuits had some initial successes, but their political meddling enraged the Abyssinian priests and by the middle of the 17th century, the Society of Jesus was banished from Ethiopia. There were no more Christian missionaries from the West until the 19th-century colonial era, when the great explorers were followed by waves of missionaries, soldiers and merchants. Explorer James Bruce's encounter with the Falashas at the end of the 18th century was to inspire a movement of British missionaries—pious Anglicans, who read his popular travel account and vowed to convert the Abyssinian Jews. The Protestant crusade began in 1809 with the founding of the London Society for the Promotion of Christianity Amongst the Jews, which aimed at converting the Jews of Africa, Europe, Asia and North America.

Samuel Gobat, who first sought out the Beta-Israel in 1830, would become the inspirational leader of the movement's effort to win over the Beta-Israel. Gobat, who later became Anglican bishop in Jerusalem, worked with several German-Jewish converts to Protestantism, including the Reverends Wolff, Isenberg, Rosenthal and the most fanatical of them all, Henry A. Stern. In 1855 Gobat sent two missionaries from Jerusalem to Ethiopia to obtain permission from Emperor Theodore to convert the Falashas. The emperor told missionaries J. F. Krapf and J. M. Flad that he was willing, but only if the Jews were baptized into the Ethiopian Orthodox Church. The Protestant felt that this proviso was not much of a concession. On the contrary, they believed that the arrangement would provide a means for reforming Ethiopian Christianity from within. Theodore gave his full support to the Church Mission to the Jews, since the emperors had been trying for centuries to convert the Falashas. One of his first gestures to the Protestants was to ban the Beta-Israel practice of animal sacrifice.

The missionaries registered further progress in 1860, when Henry Stern left his mission work in the Middle East and set out to "bring the Gospel of Christ" to the Falashas. He was ordained in Jerusalem by another apostate Jew, Bishop Michael Solomon Alexander. Stern was a quixotic Christian soldier who had labored hard to win Jewish souls in Arabia, Turkey, Baghdad and Persia. He was bent on bringing evangelical Protestantism to Jews in the remotest areas of the earth, spurred, perhaps, by his own apostasy. In 1859 the London Society provided funds for Stern to conduct an intensified mission to the Ethiopian Jews. Stern kept a rather anemic account of his Ethiopian adventures, sketching only his reception by Emperor Theodore and his visits to Falasha villages but going into depth when recounting his proselytyzing speeches to the natives. His book, *Wanderings Among the Falashas in Abyssinia*, was aimed at an English audience hungry for information about the exotic black Jews of deepest Africa.

Stern went back to England after only a few months in Ethiopia and got on the lecture circuit to raise more money for the mission. Meanwhile, his colleagues in Ethiopia were baptizing their first Falasha converts in 1862. Stern would return that year with two reinforcements: fellow German-Jewish converts Rev. Henry Rosenthal and his wife.

The missionaries were not always prepared for the work ahead of them. Two English travelers in Sudan during this time described their meeting near the Ethiopian border with two German-born missionaries from England: The missionaries had brought with them trunks full of Christian Bibles printed in Tigrean, which neither they nor the Falashas could read, and they carried a large supply of medicine that they did not know how to administer.

Henry Stern made definite headway in his second journey. He soon appointed converted Falashas as lay preachers, and he sent them out to the villages. New converts were duly baptized into the Ethiopian church, in accordance with the agreement between the CMJ and the emperor—and this practice was still being followed by the mission in the 1970s.

Stern, who was driven by messianist beliefs, told the Beta-Israel that he too was a Jew, a "white Falasha." He was outspokenly critical of Emperor Theodore and of the Ethiopian priesthood. And Stern's book, in which he criticized the emperor, soon became a *casus belli* in Theodore's quarrel with the British government. In 1864 Theodore ordered the imprisonment of all European missionaries, as well as the British counsel because, the emperor claimed, Queen Victoria had ignored a letter he had sent her. Also, he was upset that Stern's book had tarnished his reputation in England. Theodore summoned Stern to his court at Gondar, questioned him about his activities and ordered that Stern's servants be thrashed in front of the missionary. Stern nervously bit his fingers in sympathy, but this gesture to Ethiopians indicated vengefulness, and Theodore was only further enraged. Stern and another missionary were chained hand and foot and thrown into the dungeon of Magdala. Theodore used his white hostages as a trading card to demand full diplomatic relations with Britain. This was a critical goal in his overall plan to conquer Jerusalem, and thus the whole world. The emperor believed he was the messiah, and had assumed the name Theodore in order to fulfill an Ethiopian tradition that this would be the messiah's name. But Theodore was the ruler who forged modern Ethiopia, and he is still regarded as one of the greatest of Ethiopian emperors. The Falashas had mixed feelings about him. The pandemonium that accompanied Theodore's reign also led the Beta-Israel to believe that the messianic time was at hand—however, they spurned Theodore's claim to the title, for he seemed to be set against the Jews. But the Falashas also said that Theodore's mother was a Falasha, and they believed that he would not oppress them too greatly.

An anonymous Falasha writer in 1862 recorded a confrontation that took place in the presence of the emperor between the Beta-Israel's spiritual leader and Protestant missionaries and one of their Falasha converts. Wube Beru, who had been converted by Flad, implored Theodore to act against the Jews. The emperor agreed, saying, "How is it that there are people who believe not in what I believe?" He commanded that they "adopt my religion and be baptized." But a Beta-Israel holyman named Abba Simon[1] approached

---

[1]Abba, or father, is a title given to all Ethiopian priests, Christian or Jewish.

Theodore and said, "May God show you the truth" and implored him to "Give us justice." Then Abba Simon and Wube Beru debated the Bible in front of the assembled court, Jew against Christian. At one point, the Beta-Israel holy man criticized the head of the Abyssinian Church, thereby angering Theodore, who threatened: "It is I who have the power to split and cut." Abba Simon answered calmly: "It is my flesh that you can split and cut, but you cannot touch my soul." The emperor rewarded him for his courage with a gift of two fat bulls. But Theodore continued to side with the Protestants' efforts to convert all the Jews in his realm.

It was because of this religious dispute—the debate centered on concepts of the unity versus the trinity of God—that the Falashas attempted to leave en masse for Palestine.

Emperor Theodore held his thirty European hostages for more than four years, during which he engaged in constant "off with their heads" threats in negotiations with the British. Finally, Queen Victoria's government sent a military expedition of twelve thousand men to Ethiopia, led by Lord Napier. The British forces defeated the emperor's army in 1868 and drove Theodore to suicide. All of the hostages were rescued, relatively unharmed after a harrowing four years in captivity.

Henry Stern lost no time after his release, and upon his return to England he published his fourth book, *The Captive Missionary*.

DURING THE next thirty years, the mission's activities

continued unabated. Falasha converts, several of whom were trained by the church in Basle in the 1870s, manned the stations established at Jenda, Azzoza and Dagusa.

Theodore's successor, Emperor Johannes (1868-89), made another attempt to force conversion on all of Ethiopia's "heathens." The anonymous Beta-Israel writer who had described the religious dispute during Theodore's reign said that Johannes was successful with the Moslems, who had converted, and with the Woyto (Agaw hippo hunters of Lake Tana), who were baptized. But the Falashas were steadfast: "Israel refused to be baptized," he wrote.

The Italian campaign of 1896 interrupted the operations of the missionaries, who had become the emperors' instrument for eliminating "subversive" religious beliefs. After the Italians were defeated at Adowa, Emperor Menelik II, successor to Johannes, encouraged the Falasha converts to reopen the CMJ missions, which prospered until the next Italian invasion of Ethiopia two generations later. The Italians allowed only Catholic missionaries to work in Ethiopia during their six-year occupation, 1936-42. But after World War II, Emperor Haile Selassie resumed wholehearted support of the London Society for Promoting Christianity Amongst the Jews, and he welcomed back the exiled Protestant missionaries.

Ras Tafari, the man who called himself Haile Selassie ("Holy Trinity"), ruled Ethiopia as regent and emperor from 1916 to 1974. He was really the chief missionary of his feudal realm. The diminutive monarch had told several Jewish personalities over the years that he was totally opposed to allowing any of "his" people out of the country.

Even though the Beta-Israel represented only a tiny presence—twenty-eight thousand among about twenty-eight
million Ethiopians—the emperor felt that it was his mission
to convert the Jews. Haile Selassie maintained the policy of
previous Amhara emperors of using Coptic Christianity and
the Amharic language as tools to force unification among
the many disparate peoples of Ethiopia. Like Emperor
Theodore, he was also determined to unify the tribes. When
the Protestant missionaries appealed for his help in their
efforts to convert the Falashas, he gave them his active
support, with the aim of breaking down Beta-Israel society.
In some minor respects, the emperor did try to stem the
hatred directed toward the Falashas. He sponsored decrees
against the use of the blood-libel term *buda* by Ethiopian
Christians when they referred to the Beta-Israel. But it was a
token ban, impossible to enforce, and the edicts had little
effect. Whenever the matter of emigration came up, the
emperor made his position very clear—he vowed that the
Falashas would never be allowed to leave Ethiopia.

The Protestant mission flourished until Christian missionary activities were curbed by the revolutionary military
junta in the 1970s, and most of the missionaries were
expelled from Ethiopia. Just before the clampdown, one
missionary to the Jews at the Teda station was asked why he
had come from England, why was he so intent on turning
the Jews into Christians. The missionary, a cold, fey young
man, responded grudgingly to questions. He had been in
Ethiopia for two and one half years, working as a nurse in
the clinic. He and his wife refused to give any details of their
work, insisting that it was necessary to talk with the head of

the mission in Gondar, a man who had had previous experience converting Jews in Israel, Iran, England, France and the United States. But the young missionary was prodded into making one statement: He denied, in a righteous, offended manner, charges that the missionaries bribed the Beta-Israel to become Christians. "That's false," he said. "We even get fees for medical attention. We never give money—we haven't got it to give. We believe that being a Christian is the main thing—if the Falashas refuse to accept their people that become Christians, then they are wrong. We do not baptize. We teach them the Christian faith, but ultimately they'll be baptized by the Ethiopian Orthodox Church. We do not try to set up an Anglican Church."

The chief missionary in Gondar told a writer that he "hoped the Falashas would build a true Christian faith on the foundation of their traditional practices, much as Paul did."

The missionaries' medical services—clinics at Macha, Acheffer and Teda—were considered absolutely vital by even the staunchest critics of mission activities. According to an Israeli who worked with the Beta-Israel, the medical aid is "worth whatever they charge the Falashas and their neighbors." But the Beta-Israel claim that the price they paid is a great one—they were constantly pressured to convert, and tempted by promises of better education, scholarships, and an end to their job discrimination problems.

In recent years, the church mission—and a rival Seventh Day Adventist mission to the Falashas—still used converted Falashas to preach to fellow tribesmen, and proudly boasted that there were "many Hebrew Christians in the field" on four continents. In pamphlets put out regularly during the last one hundred years, the mission has promised to "break down the strongholds of Satan," the dark prince who makes the Jews of Christendom "oppose the Messiah of the New Testament." A church comic book, *Abyssinian Adventure*, features a converted Falasha boy who is determined to "win my people for Jesus Christ" even though he recognizes that this will bring "discord, strife, it may be, even the shedding of blood. It has been so in all ages of the Church. It has been so with my people from the beginning . . ." This pamphlet, issued in the 1930s, was No. 87 in a long series of "Boys' Adventures."

The missionaries are a dedicated lot; many of them spent ten, twenty or more years working in Ethiopia. In Eric Payne's missionary book, *Ethiopian Jews*, two characteristics of the missionaries are described: the "resolve to identify" with the Falashas and the "resolve to endure" the hardship of life in Ethiopia. Payne himself was a young Englishman with a curacy in Bath when he "heard God's call" and was overwhelmed by "The need to take the Gospel to the Jews." Payne, who spent more than twenty years preaching to the Beta-Israel, writes that the perfect wedding present he and his bride received was the conversion of a Falasha *cohen*. His wife is the granddaughter of the 19th-century missionary, J. M. Flad.

Payne was distressed in 1954 when "Israel established 35 schools" for the Beta-Israel in Begembdar province. But he felt that his prayers were answered when Israeli doubts about the Falashas' Jewishness finally prevailed: "Israel stopped sending any more grants . . . By 1958, there were only a few village schools left." Payne was relieved that "the Orthodox Jewish rabbis in Israel have rejected the Falashas." To his mind the mission was doing nothing but good for the Falashas, and the Israelis had threatened to delay the advance of Christianity in remote northwest Ethiopia.

Anthropologist Michelle Schoenberger holds a different view of the mission's effect on the Beta-Israel. She asserts that a Falasha who converts sells himself for a mess of pottage: "When a Falasha converts to Christianity, he believes, or rather has been led to believe, that when he is baptized into the Church and has agreed to follow the teachings of Jesus Christ, he will lose the stigma which is attached to his Falasha heritage. He also believes that he will become an Amhara after his baptism and so he will be able to marry an Amhara girl and thereby receive rights to land through his Amhara wife." But he always remains just a baptized Falasha to the Amhara. He's never accepted, and he'll rarely find an Amhara woman willing to marry him. Furthermore, his fellow tribesmen will have nothing to do with him. The convert is excommunicated—left in missionary limbo.

The Beta-Israel are extremely wary of strangers who visit their region—for they might be missionaries, or Christians disguised as Jews. Some Falashas believed that an English Jew, who served in 1974 as the representative of Jewish charities, might be an apostate Jew, like Henry Stern—he was accused of fraternizing too much with the Protestant missionaries of Gondar. And the missionaries were regarded as arch-enemies of the Falashas, because they promoted the idea that the Falashas harbored evil. Spirits wrestle the superstitious tribesmen of northern Ethiopia. Most Ethiopians, including the Beta-Israel, believe in the cult of the *zar*, a personal spirit that may be male or female, is usually malevolent, and causes terrible disease or other misfortune—most often to women between the ages of fifteen and thirty. The shamans who deal with *zars* and other spirits are called *balazar*,[2] master of the *zar*. But the missionaries state that *zar* spirits do not possess the poor people—Satan does. And the Protestant missionaries[3] have nurtured the Ethiopian belief that the Jewish Falashas are the incarnation of the spirits that torment the Chrisitans of northern Ethiopia.

AFRICA'S CHRISTIAN missionaries have often seemed as out of place, as alien, as Henry Stern. Political formulas included them in an equation with European explorers, soldiers and businessmen who together shaped the colonial experience.

The missionaries, of course, saw themselves as divinely inspired idealists, bringing civilization and God and law to the natives: Indians, Africans, Chinese, Jews. Many of them have viewed their work as a Christ-fight against Moslem missionaries, for Islam has steadily been winning Africa.

---

[2] This may be related to the Greek word for Satan, *Balthazar,* or Lord of the Flies.

[3] In the 19th century, Flad claimed that Falasha diviners possessed a "book of sorcery" called *Auda Negast,* and that Emperor Theodore forbade its use under penalty of death.

The missionaries' meddling in African tribal and national politics has been a prominent feature of their presence, but they also have saved thousands of lives with their medical skills. During the 1973-1975 drought in Ethiopia, the missionaries were among the first to get word past Haile Selassie and Western embassies of the mass starvation taking place.

Since the missionary activities were curbed in Ethiopia in 1977, Cuban doctors and nurses have gradually taken their places.

The Jewish Mission

ONE EFFECT of the Protestant missionary work in the 19th century was to bring the Falashas' situation to the attention of the Alliance Israelite Universelle in France, the *Jewish Chronicle* of London, and rabbis and Jewish leaders elsewhere in Europe.[1] The Alliance had sent Professor Joseph Halevy, a French-Jewish linguist well-known for his archeological work in Yemen, to visit the Ethiopian Jews in 1868, the year of Theodore's defeat and suicide. The Falashas who first met him were extremely distrustful and gave him a cold reception. "You know my dear brethren that I also am a Falasha!" Halevy said to them, just as Stern had said. The response to him was: "What! You a Falasha! A

---

[1]Filossemo Luzzato, the noted Italian-Jewish scholar writing in the 1840s, was one of the first to interest European Jewry in the Falashas. Luzzato's Galician contemporary and friend, Rabbi Solomon Rapoport, wrote an essay on the Jews of Ethiopia and Arabia in 1832.

white Falasha! You are laughing at us. Are there any white Falashas?" Halevy assured them that all the Falashas of Jerusalem, and in other parts of the world, were white. "The name of Jerusalem which I had accidentally mentioned changed as if by magic the attitude of the most incredulous. A burning curiosity seemed all at once to have seized the whole company. 'Oh, do you come from Jerusalem, the blessed city? Have you beheld with your own eyes Mount Zion, and the House of the Lord of Israel, the holy Temple?' . . . I must confess I was deeply moved on seeing those black faces light up at the memory of our glorious history."

Halevy learned how well-financed Protestant missionaries were winning converts, and he resolved to do something about it. The famed Orientalist returned to Paris with manuscripts, notes on his travels, and two Beta-Israel children who were to be educated in Europe. Halevy also sponsored another Falasha's rabbinical studies in Cairo.

Halevy resumed his teaching career at the Sorbonne, where two of his students took an interest in the situation of the African Jewish tribe. One of those students, Jacques Faitlovitch, would make this his life's work.

IN 1904 JACQUES Faitlovitch, an Orthodox Jew who was born in Lodz in 1880, gathered language books, maps and diplomatic documents and set out from Paris for Ethiopia's Semien mountains. Baron Edmond Rothschild and Chief Rabbi Zadok Kahn of Paris helped to finance the Sorbonne scholar's trip. In his diary of the arduous journey, Faitlovitch wrote of his first meeting with the Falashas. As was the case when Halevy had visited them 30 years before, the Falashas refused to believe that Faitlovitch was a Jew. Only missionaries used *that* trick—there were no other Jews in the world except the Beta-Israel.

Faitlovitch spent over a year with the Falashas on his first trip, living in their villages and praying in their synagogues. When he returned to Paris, he submitted a report to his patron, Rothschild: "You see, M. le Baron . . . the Falashas are really Jews. They have the same aspirations that we do; they believe, like us, that they are the future of Israel . . . They are an active, intelligent, moral people, with a thirst for learning." He ended by imploring the philanthropist to extend his humanitarian efforts to the Ethiopian Jews. But this never came about. The Alliance Israelite Universelle was not interested in helping primitive black Jews.

Faitlovitch was deeply worried by the success of the Protestant missions, and he appealed to Jews around the world to help preserve the Beta-Israel. He set up Falasha support committees in Europe and the United States to help offset the work of the missions.

Faitlovitch's efforts were undermined when the Alliance sent Rabbi Haim Nahum to Ethiopia to check on his reports. Nahum differed completely with the man who was to become the leading benefactor of the Beta-Israel. In his 1908 report, Rabbi Nahum stated categorically that the Falashas were not of Jewish blood, that they were happy where they were, and that it wasn't worthwhile to teach them modern Judaism. He went even further and paid tribute to the work of the Christian missionaries.

Faitlovitch, accusing Rabbi Nahum of being overly influenced by the Protestants, lamented the Falashas' fate, calling them "those martyrs of Judaism." And in the coming years, Faitlovitch persisted, setting up his own "mission" and stemming the tide of baptisms. The Christian missionaries at Jenda and Azozza took this as a sign of their own success, saying that their spiritual results must be impressive if a leading Jewish scholar was so concerned.

Faitlovitch spent many months teaching in Beta-Israel villages. Like Halevy, he took several Ethiopian Jews to Europe and Palestine, where he arranged for their education. In 1914 he founded a school for the Beta-Israel in Begembdar, and in the 1920s Faitlovitch and his sister, Leah, set up a teacher training school for Falashas in Addis Ababa. This boarding school was for the children of six Beta-Israel families who were brought to the capital to work for Haile Selassie as builders and blacksmiths. His sister, Leah Faitlovitch Berman of Rehovot, Israel, has said that her brother was totally obsessed by the Falashas, "His whole life was consecrated to assisting them."

During 1906-1922 Faitlovitch received aid from a Falasha support committee in Italy, which later made its headquarters in Germany. The group's activities were subsequently transferred to the American committee, which was founded in 1922 to "rehabilitate our co-religionists." Jacob Schiff, Louis Marshall, Cyrus Adler and Dr. Israel Goldstein were prominent members of the group, which held an affair in 1930 aboard a steamship to raise money for Ethiopian Jewry. A special benefit program was published, complete with ads from Bonwit Teller, Samuel Rosoff "the subway builder," and the Sisterhood Temple of Jamaica, Queens. The Women's Division chairman wrote that "The romance of the discovery of the Falashas and details of their mode of living as well as their ambitions for the future, form a fascinating story. The preservation of this remnant of the tribe of Israel is one of the strange phenomena of Jewish history. We must help them to maintain their identity . . ."

Faitlovitch was executive director of the committee, which was headed by Dr. Goldstein, the eminent rabbi.

For a period spanning fifty years, Jacques Faitlovitch helped the Beta-Israel in Ethiopia, and made frequent trips to Europe, America and Palestine to raise money for the African Jews. After the state of Israel was established in 1948, Faitlovitch, who had become an Israeli citizen, managed to persuade the Jewish Agency's Torah Education Department to send two rabbis to Asmara in Eritrea, where a boarding school for the Falashas was established. But the project was soon abandoned.

Jewish aid was skimpy. One Israeli physician was sent in the 1960s on a two-year mission to help the Falashas— and Dr. Dan Harel is still a legend among the Beta-Israel. The highland people admired Harel, a former paratrooper, because he would walk great distances up and down the steep, mountainous country, visiting the remotest Falasha villages. The people loved him. But at the end of Harel's tour of service, no one was sent to replace him. There was little medical aid from Israel for the Falashas. Israeli medical teams still served in Ethiopia, but none of this aid was designated for the Jews of Ethiopia. In the early 1970s, the

English Falasha Welfare Association sent a Jewish medical student to help the Beta-Israel. But according to an anthropologist who was living with the tribe at the time, the medical student was a "mental case," devastated by culture shock. He refused to treat patients, gave all his medicines to the government hospital in Gondar, and fled back to England.

Jacques Faitlovitch, the greatest friend and helper of the Falashas, died in Tel Aviv in 1955, bequeathing to the state his important library[1] on Ethiopia, the Beta-Israel and the lost tribes of Israel. He left his large house as a meeting place for the Israeli Falashas, and the small community gathers there for important committee meetings and for special events.

In Ethiopia, the Falashas still quote from what Faitlovitch taught them fifty years ago whenever some change in ritual is being considered.

They gave up slaughtering the paschal lamb at Passover, for example, at Faitlovitch's urging. He is honored by the Falashas more than anyone in their modern history.

The Beta-Israel support groups in England[2] and the United States are still active. Together with the Israel association headed by Professor Aryeh Tartakower, they have continued to raise funds for the Falashas and have lobbied for the tribe's immigration to Israel.

---

[1]The library was moved from Faitlovitch House to Tel Aviv University in 1975, against the wishes of the Falasha community.

[2]The English "Falasha Welfare Association" included representatives from the Jewish Colonization Association, the Jewish Agency, the American Joint Distribution Committee and the Central British Fund.

British Zionist leader Norman Bentwich and later David Kessler, publisher of the London *Jewish Chronicle*, were active in trying to raise funds for aid to the Falashas. In 1973 the British-based Falasha Welfare Association became the umbrella organization for various Jewish charities and the Jewish Agency, Israel's immigration institution. The amount of aid going to the Falashas was tiny, but it was thought that now that there was a framework, the funds would begin to flow. The FWA hired an Anglo-Jewish schoolteacher living in Addis Ababa to become the first Field Representative to the Falashas. But the Falashas didn't trust the man because he fraternized too much with the Protestant missionaries around Gondar and rarely went to the remote villages. He worked in a semi-secret manner, arousing the suspicions of the government, and the Ethiopians threw him out of the country in April, 1975. Six months later, he was replaced by Rafi Tarfon, an Israeli agriculture expert who had been working for many years in Ethiopia. His salary was $28,000 out of a budget of $66,000 in 1975—a budget that was increased to $120,000 in 1976. But Tarfon, who was the most effective emissary ever sent to the Falashas, was fired for insubordination when the international organization ORT took over aid to the Falashas with a much broader-based, $2 million non-sectarian program. The British Falasha committee, which was never overly enthusiastic about helping the Falashas to immigrate to Israel, went along with the new approach offered by ORT.

The American Association for Ethiopian Jews—headed by Graenum Berger, a long-time activist for the Falashas, and Professor Howard Lenhoff—has been the most militant of the groups in campaigning for aid to the Falashas. It has also been a bone in the throat of ORT and the other large Jewish organizations that became involved in aid to the Falashas after 1976. The American Falasha committee urged the Israeli Falashas to make their struggle public and to demonstrate in front of the prime minister's office and the Knesset, or parliament; so after years of being told that quiet diplomacy would solve their problems, the Falashas decided to follow a more activist line, and they made their protest public.

In 1978 and 1979, the American committee started receiving disturbing reports from Ethiopia about the activities of ORT. The Falashas said the ORT program was destroying their tribe faster than the attacks by rebel armies, poverty, or any other calamity in their recent history. "To our horror," the Israeli Falasha leaders wrote, "Unimaginable destruction was brought upon our community by the very organization which had come to aid us." It was the ultimate irony for the Falashas: a Jewish organization as well as the Israeli government were contributing to the destruction of the Falashas—at least, that's what they believed. It was also what they were told by an Israeli who was ORT's former field representative in Gondar, Amos Ozari. ORT had to maintain its nonsectarian program because most of the $2 million it raised for the program came in the form of grants from the Canadian, U.S., West German and Dutch governments.

Ozari said that ORT forbade him from trying to intervene on behalf of Falasha religious teachers who were arrested. "It became obvious to me what ORT's priorities really were . . . ORT's reputation was more important than peoples' lives."

Ozari said his year's work in Gondar was "a confrontation with an evil that I could never have imagined before." And he said the chief culprits were ORT's top executives in Geneva. He said he told the Falashas in Ethiopia, "don't despair, you are going to be saved."

"I misled them, I told them that something was being done even when it became obvious that nothing was being done. I became a collaborator with the policy to lull the Falashas while they're being destroyed. The leaders that we depended on were lost to us, to the Jews. They had warned of the danger. They were ready to sacrifice their lives. But nothing was done to save them. Israeli officials were indifferent to the Falasha problem, it was not a high priority matter despite their claims that it was. They treat the Falashas like children, like a burden. They tell them to keep quiet, it's being worked on, 'something' is always being done, but they won't tell the Falashas what that something is. I am haunted by what's happening."

The allegations by Amos Ozari were presented to ORT executives in New York in April, 1979, accompanied by a demand from the American Association for Ethiopian Jews for an investigation of the charges, including mishandling of funds and mistreatment of the tribe. The new president of American ORT flew to Geneva to talk to ORT's Ethiopia program chief, and his two superiors, who denied all the allegations—there were twenty-two specific charges made. The American ORT officials returned to New York and declared the allegations were "malicious and slanderous," saying that the program chief "may have talked too tough (to the Falashas), but that's all." The testimonial of Ozari and the auxiliary reports by a Falasha leader in Ethiopia and by two Swiss pottery experts were dismissed as groundless. ORT prepared a point-by-point rejoinder to the chargers, but issued only a categorical denial.

Publisher David Kessler came back from a ten-day trip to Gondar, in which he was accompanied by the ORT program director and reported that ORT was doing an excellent job. A USAID representative also visited the ORT projects, and reported that the organization was helping to reverse the tribe's degenerating situation. An informal Israeli commission of inquiry also cast doubt on Ozari's allegations, even though some of his charges were supported by other ORT employees who had been in the field in Ethiopia.

Another Israeli who had preceded Ozari in Ethiopia also condemned ORT for its program, which he said undermined the tribe's basic structure.

"The Falasha community is under permanent attack from their neighbors in a hostile environment," Rafi Tarfon wrote. "They survived through their tight, close-knit organization, by religious and tribal brotherhood—keeping their community exclusively in their own hands. For centuries, the Ethiopian emperors tried in vain to disband the Falasha community by forcing open their internal organization. Today, the close-knit Falasha community is disintegrating. Religion lost its decisive influence, especially on the younger generation. The more educated youths left the area and are frequently lost to their people. Now—absurd as this may appear—Jewish organizations may add the death blow by destroying what remains of the tribe's internal organization.

"To save Jewish money, ORT promised to enlist foreign aid (U.S., Holland, Canada, etc.). This necessitated changing the Falasha program to an Ethiopian aid project. To defend this action the story was invented that nobody would be allowed to operate in Ethiopia without changing the Falasha project into an all-out Ethiopia program. This is utter nonsense. And what the Ethiopian emperors tried to do is now accomplished by Jewish organizations, because of unbelievable erroneous judgement of the situation— aggravated by negligence and criminal carelessness."

8

Israel

The Politics of Immigration

IN ITS FIRST thirty years the Jewish national home absorbed hundreds of thousands of Jewish refugees. Most had fled from Arab countries, 100,000 were survivors of the Nazi concentration camps, and tens of thousands of others managed to flee from repressive regimes of the left and right. Israel also attracted a small number of Western Jews who might have suffered social anti-Semitism, but who couldn't be considered as refugees, or victims of authoritarian rule. In all, Israel absorbed Jews from more than seventy countries: Moroccans, Russians, Kurds, Indians, Bulgarians, Iraqis, Swedes, Peruvians, Iranians, Georgians, Rhodesians, Germans, Americans, Yemenites. The physical contrasts—and the social gaps—in this polyglot society are immediately apparent.

The leaders of the country naturally have tried to attract the more advanced immigrants—educated persons trained in the Western tradition. Among immigrants from a country like Russia, for example, Israel may consider Moscow scientists to be more valuable than Georgian laborers. American aircraft engineers are actively recruited and given special incentives—as are basketball stars. Anyone familiar with Israel's security needs cannot criticize the recruitment of aircraft technicians. But there are serious questions about some of the millions spent to attract other Jews, most of whom do not want to immigrate to Israel. For years, nothing at all was spent—and no *shaliach*, or envoy, was sent—to bring the tribe of primitive Falasha Jews on *aliyah*, the "going up" to Israel.

Over the years, Israel developed a system of priorities in immigration, and this automatically created "aberrations." It started even before Israel won independence in 1948. During World War II, Jewish Agency emissaries in Turkey were able to make deals to save the lives of a tiny number of European Jews. Those who were Labor Zionists were chosen first. In wartime, you are forced to pick who you can save from among the injured, and you pick your own. The issue is still alive. In an article on Soviet Jewish "dropouts," Abba Eban wrote: "The most satanic and heinous anti-Zionist propaganda after the Second World War sought to saddle Zionism with the sin of indifference to the saving of Jewish lives other than those destined for Eretz Israel. We dare not give retroactive validity to this libel by giving our Jewish solidarity a parochial or selective nature."

Although Eban said that only "satanists" dared to criticize the Jewish leadership (Eban has said that he was referring to "Ben Hecht and others") for its immigration policies, there obviously was and *is* a system of priorities. And the Falashas were always at the bottom of Israel's immigration ladder. If anything, their existence was a minor nuisance to the foreign policy theorists who were fashioning Israel's elaborate, ill-fated African program.

For a decade, the Labor Party government officially was "not enthusiastic" about bringing the Ethiopian Jews to Israel. Some Israeli Falashas and their supporters insist that there was criminal negligence under the Labor-led coalition in relation to Ethiopian Jews who were "on the verge of a holocaust." They claim that the issue of the Falashas was put aside because of the political relations between Haile Selassie's government and Israel. But Labor politicians deny that the subject was even brought up—it was not considered important enough to be discussed in the higher echelons.

In articles written for the consumption of American Jews, Labor politicians like Shimon Peres waxed glowingly about Israel's ingathering of the exiles, taking particular pride in the 1949-1950 Magic Carpet—the transfer of the "unique and distant Yemenite tribe" that lived in faraway mountains, cut off for hundreds of years . . .

"Those who came by plane had never seen a metal wing," he rhapsodized in an American newspaper in 1978.

The Beta-Israel were not as fortunate.

Many of the Ethiopian Jews in Israel remain bitter and cynical about the former Israeli government. "We were betrayed," says one Falasha living in the Tel Aviv area, "And even though the Begin people seem to be trying to help us, it may be too late."

No Israeli representative ever took up the cause of

Ethiopia's Jews at an international forum. One reason given
is that this might have sealed the Falashas' fate, given the
savage nature of life in Ethiopia. A more likely motive is
that Israel did not wish to offend Ethiopia. Also, the reports
that the Falashas were on the verge of extinction were not
considered to be of direct interest to Israel.

One critical Israeli politician, former cabinet minister
Shulamit Aloni, told the Knesset in early 1977 that there
had been a "conspiracy of silence" about the Ethiopian Jews,
and she blamed "racist attitudes" among National Religious
Party and Labor officials, who had missed a golden opportunity to save the Ethiopian Jews in the months after the fall
of Haile Selassie, the key figure in Israel's African policy.

Israel's Ministry for Foreign Affairs officially denies
that there was ever any "Falasha question" involved in relations with Ethiopia. Again, it was simply "not important,"
and "the issue was never raised." A few officials—on the
Africa desk, and two former envoys—were willing to
elaborate after the official Israeli decision in 1975 recognizing the Falashas as Jews. They claimed that up until the
Ethiopian break in relations with Israel in 1973, the
Falashas had been "semi-officially" recognized as Jews by
embassy personnel serving in Ethiopia. But the Beta-Israel
themselves say that they were always turned away by the
embassy and consistently were refused any help.

ABBA EBAN WAS foreign minister during the years when
Israel's Aid to Africa program was in full swing. In 1977,
three years after he had fallen into a political limbo, the
usually expansive Eban had little to say when queried about

the Falashas. As one Israeli journalist who knows Eban well said, "He'll talk free and easy about Israeli politics now, because he's fighting to get back into power, but if you ask him about something that occurred while he was minister, he'll lie through his teeth—he won't say anything about what went on during *his* tenure in office."

Eban is a man of encyclopedic knowledge, a brilliant linguist and writer who can freely compare Israeli Labor Party factions with King Lear characters. He has an incredible memory, and can quote back verbatim the brilliant conversation that spills from his lips. But like Yosef Burg, the National Religious Party boss who was interior minister when Eban was foreign minister, he pleaded a lapse in memory about the Ethiopian Jews. "I don't exactly remember if the Falashas had ever been brought up at a cabinet session . . . It seems to me that there was a ministerial meeting on the matter and the religious party people were not enthusiastic," he said in an interview. He added that his own knowledge of the Falashas was skimpy: "That is a subject on which my ignorance is vast," he chortled; "I do recall that Norman Bentwich bothered us about the Falashas. And David Kessler of London's *Jewish Chronicle* talked to me about it—I suppose it's a 'gentlemen's interest' for him. I believe the embassy used to send prayer books to the Falashas. But it was never considered to be an important issue . . . It never complicated our relations [with Ethiopia] at all."

Eban was able to recall more precisely his previous encounters with Haile Selassie, including one that had taken place more than forty years before. Eban was a leading

Cambridge scholar in 1936 when Haile Selassie, living in exile in England, was invited to dinner by a Cambridge society. Eban, who had received an acceptance note from the emperor, recalled the exact words on the incongruous letterhead: "Haile Selassie, Conquering Lion of Judah, King of Kings, Arbiter of the Ebb and Flow of the Tides; 25 Smith Street, Bath." He sat next to the emperor at that dinner, and by way of making conversation the brilliant Jewish scholar said, "Very interesting legend about Solomon and the Queen of Sheba." Haile Selassie's contemptuous reply was: "It's not a legend. It's a fact." It was the only remark he made to Eban.

In 1972 Eban made an official visit to Ethiopia, but all that he chose to relate about the trip was a bemused observation that he had been housed in a guesthouse next door to the cage where the emperor kept his old and toothless lion. Eban said he had also noticed that the parquet floor of the palace was decorated with Stars of David. But about the Falashas, nothing. In a later interview with Eban, in April, 1977, the former minister said: "I don't really know the degree of the Falashas' connection with Israeli society. I don't know much about them—but I do know that it is a very marginal problem."

Israel and Ethiopia

THE ISRAELI Foreign Ministry and the nations' leaders from Ben-Gurion on have considered Israel's links with Ethiopia to be a crucial concern. There were three main reasons for this, according to political scientist Michael Brecher: Ethiopia's prominence in Africa, her geopolitical location on the Red Sea and the Horn of Africa, and her role as a Middle East "periphery" state.[1]

Israeli officials had special hopes for Ethiopia. Shimon Peres, who became head of the Labor Alignment in 1977, spelled out in 1966 the foreign policy goals he wanted Israel to pursue during the next ten years. The very first resolve was "to build a 'second Egypt' in Africa; that is, to help convert Ethiopia's economic and military strength into a counterforce to Egypt, thereby giving Africans another focus." But after 1977, it was the Soviet Union, not Israel, that seemed to be accomplishing this aim.

Ethiopia was the cornerstone of Israel's African policy from the late 1950s, when Israel made a great effort to give aid to many newly independent African states. Agriculture experts, medical personnel, economic planners and military men were dispatched to numerous countries. Experimental farms, irrigation projects, youth centers and the creation of Ghana's shipping line were a few of Israel's contributions to Africa. "We went into Africa to teach," according to Golda Meir, "and what we taught was learned." One of the Africans who was given Israeli encouragement was Uganda's Idi Amin, who was promoted because of the leftward, anti-Israel shift of Milton Obote. But the main client was Haile Selassie, whose army as well as secret police got help from

---

[1] Israel considered Turkey, Iran, Cyprus and Ethiopia as "The Periphery"—a part of the Middle East neither exclusively Arabic nor Islamic. The Foreign Ministry wished to project this image to show that the region does not belong exclusively to the Arabs.

Israeli experts. The emperor felt he had a special, longtime connection with Israel.

After the Italian conquest of Ethiopia in 1936, Haile Selassie, his family and leading members of the nobility spent the first months of their exile in Jerusalem, and following his return to Addis Ababa six years later the emperor established his country's first modern economic links with the Jews of Palestine. After the 1956 Sinai war, when the Gulf of Aqaba was recognized as an international waterway, Israeli ships started to call at Ethiopia's Red Sea ports of Massawa and Assab, and at the railhead port of Djibouti. Along with the increase in trade, the two countries worked together to establish a large cotton farm in the Awash Valley. A meat-packing plant was set up by Israelis in Asmara, and a pharmaceutical factory was built in Addis Ababa. There were several other joint enterprises in transportation, education, agriculture, medicine and geology—and in security as well. The Israeli secret service, the Mossad, sent a small group of police officers to Addis Ababa, where they advised the Imperial Ethiopian Police in planning and organization. This followed the palace revolution in 1960, which was suppressed by the emperor. Haile Selassie had been visiting Brazil when the revolt broke out, but Israel provided him with a plane and flew him to Asmara—on the orders of Foreign Minister Golda Meir and Prime Minister Ben-Gurion himself.

"After the December, 1960, uprising against the government, they asked us for equipment as well as training—they wanted lie detectors," according to a former Israeli agent. "But Western methods just weren't suited for that God-forsaken country—if you asked a district police chief about the number of murders in his precinct, he only would be able to provide a rough estimate. 'About sixty,' he'd say."

The Israeli police agent visited the Beta-Israel once, out of curiosity. "They broke my heart," he said. "They were the poorest of the poor. I didn't think they were Jewish in the slightest way."

After the Six-Day War, Guinea was the only African state to break its ties with Israel. For Israel was quite open about the price for its aid: support in the United Nations. But by 1973 the Africans had come under increasing pressure to back the Arabs in the Middle East conflict. In the wake of the Yom Kippur War, most African countries, including Ethiopia, severed relations with the Jewish state. Israel's proud Africa effort seemed to have collapsed. But this was not true of Kenya and Ethiopia. (Kenya continued to allow El Al to fly to Nairobi, and cooperated with Israel to rescue airline passengers who were hijacked to Entebbe.) And despite the 1973 break in ties, Ethiopia refrained from jumping on the anti-Israel bandwagon, abstaining from the vote on the "Zionism is racism" resolution in the U.N., for example. The widespread Arab support for the Eritrean secessionists and the war with Arab League member Somalia were contributing factors. And in 1978 Israel was openly aiding the Marxist Ethiopian regime.

In 1973, when African support seemed to have vanished totally, the average Israeli said "good riddance," and condemned the whole concept of the Africa aid program. But Golda Meir stood by the African policy, saying that of all the projects the government had undertaken she was proudest of the technical assistance to Africa. She compared the African and Jewish experience—never mentioning the Falashas—and found common elements of oppression, discrimination and slavery. In her speeches, she would often quote from Herzl's novel, *Altneuland*, that only a Jew could comprehend the African question. "Just call to mind all those terrible episodes of the slave trade, of human beings who, merely because they were black, were stolen like cattle, taken prisoner, captured and sold," Herzl wrote. "Their children grew up in strange lands, the objects of contempt and hostility because their complexions were different . . . Once I have witnessed the redemption of the Jews, I wish also to assist in the redemption of the Africans."

But noble sentiments and the actual practice of foreign policy are worlds apart.

In 1958 when Golda Meir was foreign minister, she visited Liberia and noted the incredible gap between the tiny elite around President Tubman and the rest of the population, which lived in destitution. "But I hadn't come to Africa to preach, interfere or to convert," Meir wrote in *My Life*. Tubman was a "friend of the Jews" and Golda let herself be "charmed and interested" in the interior of the country, which is mostly a single, mammoth Firestone rubber plantation. Meir recounted her meeting with an old woman in the West African hellhole who simply could not believe that her visitor had come from Jerusalem—a place she thought was in heaven. "You mean, there's a *real* city?" the woman asked, thrilling Mrs. Meir.

Golda Meir was a consistent opponent of Falasha

immigration to Jerusalem. "Golda used to say that they would be miserable here, objects of prejudice," according to Rabbi Zeev Gotthold of the Ministry of Religion. Another source claims that Mrs. Meir had told her: "Don't we have enough problems? What do we need these blacks for?" It was during her years as prime minister that the government was officially "not enthusiastic" about helping Ethiopia's Jews. The issue was shelved. The Falashas were considered too primitive to become Israelis. More importantly, it was considered a mistake to offend the emperor, who was violently opposed to letting the Beta-Israel go.

"The Israeli government did not wish to do anything that would offend the emperor," according to Rabbi Israel Goldstein, who visited Haile Selassie in 1969. "The Jewish Agency never helped the Falashas because the emperor was opposed to their leaving and demanded that any aid to them be matched in kind with aid to their neighbors."

The emperor thought the Beta-Israel tribe was like a finger in Ethiopia's dike—if one tribe leaked out, all of the various peoples would clamor for independence, and the fragile empire would collapse. Israel went along with this, allowing the dust to pile up on the Falasha file while making an all-out effort to win friends in Africa. Because of the vital political link to Ethiopia, Israeli officials were willing to sacrifice a tribe whose claim to Jewishness hadn't been properly adjudicated. Israeli diplomats were frank in admitting that Israel's relations with Ethiopia were far too important to risk over the issue. But for public consumption, the Foreign Ministry claimed that "Israel has never conducted diplomatic relations with another nation at the expense of the local Jewish community, especially if it involves the right of *aliyah*." The line changed after Ethiopia cut relations in 1973. After that, Jewish Agency officials said it was *technically* impossible to help the Falashas—for example, by giving them money to pay their fares to Israel. "It's an administrative problem now—we have no embassy there now—it's a vicious circle," Jewish Agency executive Yehuda Dominitz said in 1974.

The myth that the Falashas still counted as a force in the ancient Christian-Moslem struggle for Ethiopia was perpetuated by an Israeli government leader in the 1950s. The late Yisrael Yeshayahu, longtime speaker of the Knesset, visited Ethiopia and the Falashas and issued a report on his findings. He stated that "the Ethiopian government is supported mainly by the Christian community, and apparently, any part of the population that is not Moslem (i.e., the Falashas) is likely to strengthen this support. Perhaps it is for this reason that there is much pressure brought to bear on the Falashas—not by the government, but by the Christian community—to convert to Christianity and to cease being different."

Yeshayahu, who had walked to Palestine from his native Yemen in 1929, thought that this mass conversion would solve the problem: "The government and the Christian community would be very happy and the Falashas would only stand to benefit from such a move; e.g., they would receive their own region."

This top Israeli official was not the first to suggest that the solution to Ethiopia's Jewish problem was that the Falashas convert. And he wasn't the last to argue that a handful of weak tribesmen could make a difference in the balance between Ethiopia's Christians and Moslems—twenty years after his report, some Israeli officials were still using the same notion as a rationale for ignoring the Falashas' cry for help. But two former ambassadors admitted that this "political problem" was not necessarily the primary obstacle to Beta-Israel emigration. They focused instead on the issue of whether or not the tribe is Jewish. "I agree with Ullendorff's views—the Jewishness of the Falashas is exaggerated," one diplomat said, "because other Ethiopians have Jewish traditions as well: *kashrut*, circumcision, and they build their churches on the model of the Second Temple. It would be a tragedy to bring the Falashas to Israel . . . but then, it would be a tragedy to leave them." The second envoy said: "The problem is not to kill them through the weight of love. Some of the campaigners for Falasha *aliyah* are talking complete nonsense. For example, there is absolutely no comparison with the Yemenites, who had such strong and ongoing links with Judaism. And what's happening to the Falashas in Ethiopia is not a life-or-death situation. After all, they are blacks, just one of hundreds of minorities. In many ways, they are better off than their neighbors."

Eventually, the Israeli government was stirred into taking some action to help the Falashas, following a decision by an interministerial committee in 1975. The committee officially recognized the Falashas as Jews, entitled to automatic citizenship under the Law of Return. But the first attempt to bring a small group of Falashas to Israel was aborted: There was a foulup immediately after the government announcement when the press was told that seventy Falashas would be flown to Israel within the week, the first of several flights to be paid for by the Jewish Agency. As soon as the news reached the Ethiopians, they put the clamps on the whole operation.

One Absorption Ministry official in Jerusalem expressed shock that the government committee's decision had not been kept secret. He told an interviewer that the public announcement was "stupid, wrong and dangerous to the Falashas during a period of uncertainty in Ethiopia." Other, more cynical observers thought that it might have been more than stupidity. "The government's decision may have come too late to really help the Falashas anyway, but the public announcement of it served to totally undermine the original intention—it made it impossible for the Falashas to get to Israel, and it may have sealed their fate," claimed one official who had dealt with the matter. He hinted that there might have been a conscious or unconscious attempt by some other officials to sabotage the whole plan.

Just before the 1975 government decision, Jewish Agency executive Yehuda Dominitz had this to say: "Take a Falasha out of his village, it's like taking a fish out of water . . . we are told that the *aliyah* potential is tiny—the number that would leave is minute. Most of the ones that came to Israel felt lost and they went home. I'm not in favor of bringing them." But two years later, after Dominitz had been put in charge of the immigration effort, he said that he had "changed his mind."

In February, 1978, when Foreign Minister Moshe Dayan announced to the world that Israel was arming

Ethiopia, he effectively ended the Beta-Israel's chances to emigrate from Ethiopia. Observers were dumbfounded by Dayan's "slip of the tongue"—what possible good could it do for Israel to boast about the aid? The Communist *World Marxist Review* applauded the reaction by the Ethiopian Foreign Ministry, which had termed Dayan's statement as "provocative, subtly timed." The Communists discerned a complex plot "between Israel and Arab reaction" that would be used as a pretext for direct intervention in Ethiopian events. (The Ethiopians would come to believe the Israel-Egypt peace treaty was a U.S. plot against their country.)

Some Israeli officials said that Dayan's boast was simply a thoughtless gaffe. Officials in the Prime Minister's Office, in private, also expressed dismay—for Dayan had destroyed their efforts to bring some Falashas to Israel, or so they said.

In Israel, mention of Diaspora Jews living in countries where the Jewish community is endangered falls under the censorship laws. Articles dealing with the Jews of Syria or Russia, for example, have had to be submitted to the Israeli military censor for years. After the premature announcement in 1975 that the Falashas were being flown to Israel, the subject of the Falashas was also put under the province of the military censor. There had been almost unanimous agreement among Beta-Israel supporters, including several of those who are highly critical of Israel's efforts, that the whole subject would have to be treated with the utmost care, since the Falashas live in a brutal world, where it is nothing to liquidate a tribe of only twenty-eight thousand. But there was also criticism of the censorship itself. Some felt it simply made it easier for Israel to suppress the matter and to delay taking any major action to save the Falashas. Several supporters of Falasha *aliyah* believed it had taken a scandalously long time for the issue to come to the attention of government leaders, and with the whole matter kept secret there would be no way to check up on the government's efforts.

The censor's pencil was at work after 1975, and little information about the Falashas got out: Even a one-line item was removed from a feature article about an Israeli-made film—the fact that Israeli Falashas had played the role of some Ugandan soldiers in a movie about Entebbe. In early 1979, there seemed to be a profound change in censorship policy—after the three hundred Israeli Falashas demonstrated in front of the prime minister's office and the Knesset, there was a spate of articles about the Falashas in the Israeli press. Items that undoubtedly would have been censored before were now allowed to get through. The first mention of two thousand Falasha dead or wounded was made in the press, quoting a talk by the Jewish Agency's Yehuda Dominitz.

Rabbis, Judges and Politicians

THE BETA-ISRAEL have struggled for decades to get a rabbinical stamp of approval on their Jewishness—the 1975 ministerial decision was an entirely secular action—and the question of their religion was one of the major stumbing blocks in their fight to immigrate to Israel.

The Ethiopian Jews adopted many Christian and animist beliefs during the long centuries of isolation from their coreligionists, and this brought them into conflict with modern Jewish law regarding marriage. Some rabbis categorically rejected the Falashas' claims to Jewishness, but other prominent rabbis disagreed: In 1972 Israel's chief rabbi of the Sephardi community, Ovadia Yosef, ruled that the Falashas are "undoubtedly of the Tribe of Dan . . . and their verdict is the same as that of a (Jewish) baby found amongst the *goyim* and we are ordered to compensate them and revive them."

In making his decision Rabbi Ovadia cited the opinions of several eminent sages, *g'dolim* of Israel: Avraham Yitzhak Ha'Kohen Kook, Eretz Israel's first and foremost chief rabbi; former Chief Rabbi Yitzhak Herzog; the 19th-century German Rabbi Azriel Hildesheimer, founder of Agudat Israel, and most importantly, the 15th-century Radbaz of Egypt, David Ben Zimra.

Rabbi Ovadia's ruling was supported by Israel's great Talmudic scholar, Rabbi Adin Steinzalz, a red-haired, pot-bellied genius whose work has achieved worldwide recognition. Steinzalz got involved in the Falasha question in the 1960s, at the instigation of former Knesset member Haim Ben-Asher, who had tried to force the issue with Israel's labyrinthine religious bureaucracy, the Rabbinate. "But the Rabbinate evidently was pressured by the government not to pursue the subject," Steinzalz said in an interview, "So they didn't want the question of their Jewishness opened up." Rabbi Steinzalz wanted to "force some *halachic* (Jewish legal) discussion" about the Beta-Israel, "But all I got were evasions—they just did not want to deal with it at the time."

Steinzalz' own opinion is that the Beta-Israel may have

learned their Judaism from the Jews of Elephantine, who also had lost all of their Hebrew with the exception of a few words. "The fact that Hebrew is not their holy tongue by itself creates a very great difference in perception between them and other Jews; and they will have great trouble if they ever come to Israel," he said. But he agreed wholeheartedly with Ovadia Yosef's decision that the Falashas are Jews: "The Radbaz, Rabbi David Ben Zimra, was quite clear about this, while Rabbi Kook was not as comprehensive. The Radbaz said that the Falashas are basically Jews, with strange customs. This is sufficient, all that is needed. It is a first-class decision."

The Radbaz, who was born in Spain and died at age ninety-four in Safad, Palestine, was chief rabbi from 1541 to 1554. In his ruling on the legitimacy of the son of a Falasha woman slave and her Egyptian master, he declared that the Falashas are like the Karaites, a dissident sect of Judaism, but that they—unlike the Karaites—could be accepted as Jews if they underwent instruction in Jewish laws and customs. "It is clear that they are of the seed of Israel, of the tribe of Dan, which dwells in the mountains of Ethiopia."

Three hundred years later, Berlin's Chief Rabbi Hildesheimer, one of the leading Orthodox figures of the 19th century, cited the Radbaz' decision and appealed for recognition of the Beta-Israel's Jewishness. Chief Rabbi Kook's statement on the Falashas, made in 1921, called on world Jewry "to save our Falasha brethren from extinction." He declared that it was a holy obligation to rescue the Falashas, who were "holy souls of the House of Israel." After the state was established in 1948, Chief Rabbi Herzog ruled that the Falashas were descendants of converts.

And Rabbi Ovadia Yosef's declaration was a synthesis of all these previous opinions. It meant that the Beta-Israel could be regarded as the Marranos—Spanish and Portuguese Jews forced to convert during the Inquisition but still secretly practicing Judaism; or as the Beduin youth, who had been abducted from his Jewish parents when he was an infant. They are still Jews, and the rabbis say it is a *mitzva*—a commandment—to save them: ". . . I've decided that they are Jews that should be saved from assimilation," Ovadia Yosef wrote. He called for their immediate immigration to Israel, where they would receive instruction in the Torah and "take part in the building of our holy state." He said he was "certain" that government institutions and the Jewish Agency would "do their best to assist us in this holy mission . . . the *mitzva* of saving the souls of our brothers."

Shortly after Rabbi Ovadia Yosef's decree, the chief rabbi of the Ashkenazi community, Shlomo Goren—who has been engaged in a long and bitter personal conflict with his Sephardic counterpart—told reporters he accepted "taking care of the rapid conversion of all Falasha immigrants." It seemed to signify that he, too, was in favor of bringing the Beta-Israel to Israel. But later he expressed his reservations, which further delayed concrete action by the government.

The Falashas who were already living in Israel agreed—under protest—to undergo a modified conversion to satisfy those rabbis who still had their doubts. They had to go through this conversion because their marriage customs did not conform with the Jewish law, and therefore there was a question of their legitimacy.

But Rabbi Goren and his National Religious Party

supporters in Israeli politics kept the question of the tribe's Jewishness from resolution—a portentous delay made in the name of religion.

RABBINICAL OPPOSITION to the recognition of the Falashas as Jews had been upheld by Israel's judiciary in 1968, when the Supreme Court made its landmark ruling on the Rabbinate's refusal to register a Falasha for marriage. The court found that the Jerusalem Rabbinical Council was "justified in blocking the marriage of Benyamin Gitya and the woman of his choice." Gitya, a long-time resident and citizen of Israel who had been brought to a kibbutz at an early age, always regarded himself as a Jew. His defense counsel argued that there was no room for doubting the Jewishness of the Falashas in general, and of his client in particular.

Matters of marriage and divorce for Jews in Israel are under the exclusive jurisdiction of the rabbinical courts, even though most Israelis are not observant. The rabbis insist on this right, to "guard the Jewish people against undermining by mixed marriages," improper conversion and mumzerim," children of adulterous unions. And so it is the rabbis who determine "Who Is a Jew." But the civil courts of appeal, up to the high court, can rule on decisions by the court of rabbis.

The three Supreme Court justices did not agree with Benyamin Gitya that it is sufficient for a person to declare himself Jewish in order to be recognized by the courts as such. Gitya's argument—that his declaration of Jewishness put the burden of rebuttal on the rabbinical council—was also dismissed. The court ruled that the registration clerk at the Rabbinate office had been entitled to examine Gitya's credentials and to refer him to the rabbinical court, which had decided that Gitya would have to undergo immersion in water—known as conversion "in the doubt"—before he could have a Jewish marriage.

One justice said that since the prevailing opinion held the Falashas to be converted Jews, any doubts could be removed by the immersion ceremony. Two justices said that even if the Rabbinate had erred in its interpretation of *halacha*—Jewish law—it was beyond the competence of the High Court to interfere. But Justice Witkon added that the field of *halacha* could not be completely closed to the secular courts, and therefore, the marriage clerk's refusal to register Gitya was a subject for examination by the Supreme Court.

On the Jewishness of the Falashas in general, the court declared that all of them should be reconverted by immersion in the *mikva*, or ritual bath—and circumcision when necessary—a stand the court characterized as "very liberal and lenient." For if the Beta-Israel had been found to be descended "from Jewish seed," and not from converts, then they would have been "tainted with bastardy" because their divorces were not performed strictly according to Jewish law. And they would have been prohibited from marrying Jews.

The court dismissed the defense's argument that Gitya was a Jew because his father had converted, studied at rabbinical colleges in Italy and Jerusalem and had returned to Ethiopia to teach Hebrew and Bible. This was not sufficient proof of Jewishness: "This argument obviously begged the question of the mother's conversion—which was the decisive

consideration," the court ruled. Since Gitya did not provide
any evidence of his mother's conversion, both the Rabbinical
and Supreme Courts considered his Jewishness to be in
doubt. This was a crucial point. Under the Law of Return, a
Jew is defined as being born of a Jewish mother. It doesn't
matter if the father is Jewish or not.

Justice Witkon said that the Rabbinate had adopted
the attitude that the Falashas are converted Jews "in order to
make things easier" for Gitya and had demanded that he be
immersed only to "overcome all doubts as to his mother's
conversion." But he also criticized the Rabbinate for
"pedanticism" regarding the Jewishness of Gitya's mother.
"It is not usual to make so meticulous an inspection of the
antecedents of immigrants to Israel from Western Europe
and America," even though some of these families had
"reached the verge of assimilation," he stated. The president
of the court, Chief Justice Agranat, noted that there was a
two-fold doubt about Falasha Jewishness: the sociological
question of whether the Falashas are descended from the
House of Israel or are descendants of converts, and the religious question of whether their beliefs conform with the
Jewish religion. Agranat said the prevailing view seemed to
be that the Beta-Israel are descended from converted Jews,
"although some authorities defend the theory that they are
descended from Jewish stock." He said religious doubts
stem from the fact that the Falashas do not follow the oral
law—the Talmud—"of which they are ignorant." In Gitya's
case this proved decisive, since the Falashas "apparently did
not observe the exact rules of marriage and divorce laid
down in the oral law." Agranat concluded by saying that the
Rabbinate "recognizes and appreciates what is due to the
Falashas for their zealous and courageous struggle to pre-

serve their Jewish faith and religion, as they understand it, and for this reason wished to do everything in its power to bring them into the fold of observant Judaism."

In Israel, the problems related to intermarriage are of extreme importance, since, as historian Howard Sachar observed, "by affecting one's *national* Jewishness it infinitely bedevils the *religious* rights of Israeli Jews." He cited the Gitya case as an example. "The Falashas, it appeared, were suspected by the Rabbinate of having intermarried in Ethiopia generations before, and therefore since they weren't Jewish by *nationality* (ethnic identification), they were not entitled to Jewish *religious* rights."

Like the Beta-Israel, the eight thousand Indian Jews of Israel, the B'nei Israel, did not have a rabbinical tradition but followed Mosaic Judaism. In 1961 the Rabbinate decided they were Jews, but demanded an intensive examination into the background of any Indian Jew wishing to marry another Jew. The B'nei Israel protested vehemently and demonstrated against this discrimination. After the intervention of Prime Minister Levi Eshkol and various Knesset members, the Rabbinate eventually backed down.

THE ISSUE OF THE Beta-Israel may have been raised in the Israeli cabinet under the Labor government—it's difficult to know. One ex-minister said, "I think so"; another stated, "I don't recall." A third politician said it was discussed in the cabinet and alleged that Religious Affairs Minister Yitzhak Raphael had offered this assessment: Israel doesn't need the *schvartzes*.

Until 1977, Raphael was a powerful leader of the Mafdal, the National Religious Party, which usually holds around ten seats in the one hundred twenty-member

Knesset but which has always enjoyed far-reaching power as the principal coalition partner in Israeli governments. The NRP was temporarily separated from the ruling Labor Party during a coalition crisis in late 1976, and six months later the Mafdal found a niche in the new government led by Menachem Begin's Likud. The Mafdal has grown used to dipping into the political porkbarrel, and its share under Labor included three important ministries: Religious Affairs, Social Welfare, and the Interior Ministry. The Beta-Israel's case was spread among these fiefdoms, as well as among three other government bodies: The Foreign Ministry, the Absorption Ministry, and the Jewish Agency.

In April, 1975, representatives of all these bodies met together, and declared that the Falashas are Jews under the Law of Return, entitling the Beta-Israel to immediate Israeli citizenship. The committee urged that their immigration be facilitated.

Until that interministerial decision, there was no single address or official in charge of the "Falasha problem." But in 1977 the matter came under the exclusive control of Israel's citadel of bureaucracy, the Jewish Agency. Later it would come under the province of the Prime Minister's Office.

In March, 1977, Acting Interior Minister Shlomo Hillel issued an official government statement reaffirming the 1975 decision to recognize the Beta-Israel as Jews.

When asked to comment on the two-sentence statement, Hillel would only say that "It's the Jewish Agency's problem." The terse official statement had been made in response to a charge in the Knesset that there was a continuing "conspiracy of silence" about the Falashas. Former cabinet minister Shulamit Aloni, head of the tiny Citizens'

Rights Party, had accused the government of refusing to
recognize the Falashas as Jews. She claimed that it had
buckled under to pressure from Raphael, Dr. Yosef Burg,
and other religious party figures. Aloni, who is an implacable foe of the religious parties, says that she was once joined
in her efforts on behalf of the Beta-Israel by Knesset members Mordechai Ben-Porat and Shlomo Hillel, both of whom
are Oriental Jews, refugees from Iraq. But she said that they
"did not take any initiative when it could have paid off—
during the short time that the NRP was out of the cabinct.
Now, it's too late." Aloni said that other Knesset members,
such as Esther Herlitz and Shlomo Rosenne, had told her
that the issue should be kept secret, since the Falashas' lives
were endangered. "I told them that it was only being kept
secret because Raphael thinks they're *schvartzes*," Aloni said.
Critics of Shulamit Aloni said that she was ignorant of the
tribe's real situation, and that she would "try to make
political capital out of anything—and at anybody's expense."

   Charges of racism regarding the Falashas were also
made in the press. A simplistic and somewhat inaccurate
article by Dominique Torres in *Le Monde* implied that Israel
was a racist state because it ignored the Falashas' cry for
help. Israeli officials immediately attacked the article in the
French newspaper, which is often hostile to Israel. The article's blanket accusations, and the counter-attacks it inspired, tended to obscure the issue—*some* officials definitely
had shown racist attitudes concerning the Falashas, although other Israelis, including government officials, had
fought to win the Beta-Israel recognition as Jews and to
bring them to Israel. In one Jewish organization report
shortly after the "clearly biased" article appeared, it was

conceded that the "aspersions on Israel's attitude to certain immigrant groups" contained "more than just a bit of the truth."

Yitzhak Raphael admits that he had "misgivings" about the 1975 decision to speed the immigration of the Falashas, but he denies, not surprisingly, that he was opposed to the Ethiopian Jews on racial grounds. Raphael said the whole matter was a purely *halachic* decision—the province of religious, not secular, authorities.

The National Religious Party itself never brought up the issue of Beta-Israel immigration. One reason was that the "wrong" chief rabbi was the main religious patron of the Falashas. For it was the *Sephardi* chief rabbi who had decided to recognize the Beta-Israel as Jews. In most instances, anything favored by Sephardi Rabbi Ovadia Yosef is opposed by Ashkenazi Rabbi Goren, who has much more influence with the religious politicians. Goren's aversion to Ovadia Yosef, which is mutual, is sometimes the overriding factor in Israeli religious affairs, although this is denied by Mafdal spokesmen.

While Goren made some token "conversions in the doubt" of Falashas, he stated publicly that the Beta-Israel are not Jews. According to the NRP newspaper, Goren cited the 1968 Supreme Court decision—not any religious source—for his opinion. Goren felt impelled to go on Israel television the night that the landmark secular decision recognizing the Falashas was announced. He criticized it, saying that it was up to the Chief Rabbinate to decide whether the Falashas should be regarded as Jews. What Rabbi Goren left unstated is the fact that he *is* the Chief Rabbinate. The Rabbinate in itself cannot effect the basic, secular decision recognizing the Beta-Israel as Jews despite the fact that the "Who Is a Jew" controversy falls under both the political and religious establishments—which are intertwined in complex, often baffling ways. It can, however, block the implementation of almost any measure that it opposes. Goren's influence reaches beyond the religious politicians. Labor Party politicians like former Justice Minister Haim Zadok quoted Goren's "grave doubts regarding the Falashas' identity" in order to ward off critical questions in the Knesset. But Goren's main source of power comes from the NRP bosses, especially from Mafdal leader Yosef Burg. Interior Minister Burg and Yitzhak Raphael shared a similar outlook—both were contemptuous of the Falashas. Burg denies that he helped to lead the fight against bringing the Beta-Israel to Israel. "It was never brought up in the cabinet," he said in an interview in January, 1977, shortly after his party was temporarily thrown out of the ruling coalition. "I don't exactly remember where or when it *was* brought up; but they are not Jews in the strict sense," he said with certainty. "I don't know who they are. I first of all would have to study the matter."

He said this twenty months *after* the government, including the director-general of his own ministry, had ruled that the Beta-Israel are Jews.

Burg, who claims he was acquainted with "one or two Falashas" who were studying in Leipzig, Germany, in 1933, said that he was "out of the country" at the time Minister Raphael challenged the 1975 committee's findings, and therefore, he "knew nothing about it." But he agreed with Rabbi Goren: "It's not a government matter or a party matter—it belongs to the Rabbinate."

In essence, Burg, one of the government officials charged with implementing the decision recognizing the Falashas' right to immigrate, was deciding on his own to hand the matter over to Rabbi Goren, who he knew would bury it.

He made no effort to hide his contempt for the Ethiopian Jews. "You could just as well write a book about the Martians," he said disdainfully. (When this remark was published in a 1979 article I wrote for the *Jerusalem Post*, Burg denied he had ever said it to me.)

During the 1977 Knesset election, the NRP's ad campaign featured a photograph of Burg saying, "You and I have met . . . when we organized Aliya Bet and the escape from southern France and Italy . . . On the long journeys from Africa to Israel . . ." But he obviously wasn't referring to black Africa.

In January, 1979, ex-Minister Raphael wrote an article for the newspaper *Yediot Aharanot* that flabbergasted all who knew his previous record. Calling the Falashas "our brethren," he urged an all-out effort to bring them to Israel. He concluded that the government was dragging its feet, "perhaps because of the color of their skin."

There are many observant Israeli Jews outside of the religious and political establishments who have called for the immigration of the Beta-Israel on the grounds that it is a religious imperative. Haim Lacob, a young South African-born teacher on a religious settlement, Massuot Yitzhak, taught Judaism and Hebrew to two small groups of young Falashas who arrived in Israel in the early 70s. "The Falashas are bright, good people—I depend on them for my *minyen* (prayer quorum of ten)," he said, "And the country needs them."

THE FALASHA issue in Israel has been complicated in the public's mind by the continuing problem of the "Black Hebrews" or "Black Israelites," a menacing cult of

American former Black Muslims who settled in the Negev Desert in the early 1970s, claiming to be the only "real Jews." Israelis, in their eyes, are imposters, who should be dispossessed.

They became a surreal sideshow for those who were trying to force some action on Falasha immigration. At a Jerusalem political meeting that had nothing to do with the issue, a heated argument broke out between two groups of blacks in the audience—one wearing yarmulkes, the other dressed in dashikis. The rest of the audience, white middle-class Jews, sat in amazement while the two black groups yelled abuse at each other over the issue of "Who is a Jew." The religious blacks were converts who had studied Torah in New York before immigrating to Israel, where they were accepted and recognized as Jews under the Law of Return. Many of them were continuing their studies in the religious schools—*yeshivot*—of Jerusalem.

The other group of American blacks, who had no roots whatsoever in Judaism, expressed anti-Semitic and anti-Israel sentiments. They had come to Israel from Detroit and Chicago and settled in Negev development towns, especially Dimona, despite the fact that they had no residence permits. Their leader spouted admiration for Hitler.

But when they first arrived—the original group of thirty came in 1971—they were admitted with open arms by surprised Israeli officials, in marked contrast to the reception accorded any Falasha who tried to get into Israel.

The group soon grew to five hundred, as other members of the sect entered the country disguised as pilgrims. Many of them had criminal records in the United

States, and their guru-leaders used threats and blackmail to control their followers.

The Israeli government did not take any action against these intruders, since it could prove to be "embarrassing" for the country's image if they were thrown out. The cult leader, who tried to get the U.N. to condemn Israeli "racism" directed at his group, proclaimed himself the messiah and promulgated rambling, incoherent hate literature featuring classic anti-Semitic slanders. Some group members were arrested in a holdup, another was killed by fellow members and there were other serious crimes. But they got a generally good press in Israel; the sect formed a rock group that became fairly well-known throughout the country, and a friendly, uncriticial documentary film about them was shown by Israel television. The average Israeli made no differentiation between the various groups of blacks in Israel: the one hundred or so American blacks who had legitimately converted, the three hundred Falashas, and the "Black Hebrews," whose number had grown to fourteen hundred by 1979.

The mayor of Dimona and town leaders pleaded with the government to take action against the sect, which had brought the social situation "near explosion." More and more so-called Black Hebrews joined their fellow believers, some of whom were living thirty to each tiny two-room apartment provided by the government. But the authorities, who have been immobilized on this issue for years, delayed taking action. It was the responsibility of Interior Minister Yosef Burg. Burg, who was so vigilant in opposition to Falasha immigration, made no move against the "Black

Hebrews." The damage they did to Israel and to the Falashas
was much more serious than it appeared. In America, the
sect has had continuing coverage in the black media, and a
large number of American blacks believe that the sect is
being persecuted in Israel because of color prejudice.
They've never heard of the Beta-Israel. Many American Jews
confuse the problem of the Falashas with the cult group.
They don't know the difference.

The Falashas themselves campaigned to have the
Detroit sect expelled. In a letter to the *Jerusalem Post* in
1977, a Falasha named Yitzhak Levy wrote: "The fate of
those Negroes who came from America and call themselves
Black Hebrews is being discussed again. They have caused
many problems, and they are making it hard on us Falashas
in Israel and abroad. Not only are people confused about
who is who, but it seems that no less than four times a
month, I run into a new group of these Black Hebrews, and
when I let them know where I stand, I'm given the
treatment: I'm told that I'm a traitor, an Uncle Tom, a
follower of the white man's religion, etc. If the Israeli
government is strong, it would take decisive action. And it
would also do more to help Falasha Jewry. We are Jews just
like any Jew from any part of the world. We are no
different."

But the Begin government, with Burg continuing as
Interior Minister, finally gave in to the demands of the
Dimona sect in 1979, and gave them permanent housing in
the Negev.

THE FALASHAS in Israel never were granted a meeting

with Labor Party ministers, but this changed under the Likud, and Begin himself held three long conferences with representatives of the Falasha community. In January, 1979, four Falasha leaders demanded a clear commitment from the prime minister "to evacuate immediately our people." They emphasized the urgency of the issue, the critical situation that the tribe was facing. Begin told them: "First, there is no question about your Jewishness; you are our brothers, our flesh and blood. So the Israeli government has done, is doing and will continue to do its best in searching for ways to bring our brothers here to their homeland. We are fully aware of their plight, so we will not let our brothers suffer, but the critical problem is lack of direct connections with the Ethiopian leader. Despite this, we work very hard to save the Falashas."

Begin wouldn't go further in giving a commitment. He asked them not to publicize the Falasha problem, saying that it would affect actions that were under way. But the Falashas refused. They'd heard it all before—from Yehuda Dominitz of the Jewish Agency, who was at the meeting, and from others. Two days after their meeting, two hundred Falashas demonstrated outside the prime minister's office during a cabinet session. Begin's chief aide, Eliahu Ben-Elissar, came out to assure the Falashas that "a great deal" was being done, and he also told them it was not good to speak out publicly. "Rely on the government," he told them. Later in the day, Absorption Minister David Levy was asked by an Israel radio reporter about the Falasha demonstration. He said: "Today, the government dealt with our brothers' (the Falashas) plight. We are doing and continue to do much to bring our brothers." He condemned the demonstration as "unnecessary and irresponsible."

The Falashas pressed on, meeting with various government officials—Histadrut chief Yeruham Meshel, Knesset Speaker Itzhak Shamir, Knesset member Geula Cohen—and talking to the press. A delegation of Falasha women met with Begin's wife, Aliza, and she promised to intervene in saving their families. Meanwhile, the bad news kept coming in: Falasha leaders were killed, missing, or in prison, six Falashas who had worked for an Israeli company "disappeared." And the Israeli Falashas warned: "A flock without a shepherd is nothing . . . Everything will be lost."

As the months passed, the Israeli Falashas became convinced that the Begin government was little better than the Labor regime—both governments relied on the same Jewish Agency bureaucrats and National Religious Party ministers. And the Falashas were convinced that these people were not in the business of answering prayers.

9

A Tribal Remnant

Judith's Wedding

JUDITH YALO HAD a hard time getting to know Israelis, to understand their behavior, their *chutzpah*. She thought they'd never get to know her and that she'd never get close to them. When she first came to Israel in 1972, Judith was taken to a kibbutz *ulpan* (Hebrew school) by her older sister, Ruth, who had come to Israel in the 1950s. The people at the kibbutz, near Ashkelon, liked her and were good to her and she felt they were leading a good life. But the seventeen-year-old black girl thought she wouldn't try to stay in Israel past the six months allowed on her tourist visa.

After the five-month *ulpan* was finished, Judith left the kibbutz. She wanted to take some courses but had no money, so she went to work in an electric light factory in Herzilya. It was terrible pay—about six hundred Israeli lirot a month (then, about $125), but she tried to put some money away. Judith, Ruth and a friend shared an apartment, which was subsidized by the government. She worked days and took evening classes for four months. When Judith finished the course, she took a second job at the Daniel Tower Hotel as a waitress in the cafe and later as a clerk in the accounting department. She would get up before dawn, work till 4 o'clock in the afternoon at the factory, take the bus home for a one-hour break till 5:30, then work from 6 to midnight at the hotel. She kept up the pace for seven months, getting a maximum of five hours sleep every night. Money was the motivation—Judith felt she had to make enough to send for her family; for after she had overcome the initial shock of Israel she knew she would stay and her family would follow. The situation in Ethiopia was terrible and she feared that it would get worse. She had no time or energy for a social life, no time to go to a movie or to visit friends.

David Bromberg, a metalworker, got a job with the maintenance staff of the hotel where Judith worked. They saw each other on the bus a few times, and he would say "Hello." David kept wandering around to where Judith was working, and she liked him.

Her sister's reaction to David was, "What are you doing, taking up with an Israeli boy? And a Pole on top of that!" Her friends joined the chorus and advised her not to marry him.

The same thing was happening to David. His friends would ask, "Are you crazy, marrying an Ethiopian, a black?" Pressure came from his parents. His father told him, "Judith is a good girl, very nice, but she's black." David replied, "Are you marrying her? It's my concern." His mother, at first, constantly yelled about it to his father. Later, she said, "All right," and his father said, "No."

David told Judith all about it, saying: "What can they do, disown me?"

She answered, "Look, it can only work one way. If you want it, it'll be. And if you don't want it, I don't want it. Look for someone else—I don't want to make problems with your family." She told him to decide; and he did. Judith knew he was serious and she said: "You're all right. I'll marry you."

The wedding took place in a drab meeting hall for new immigrants in Herzilya. It was an Israeli wedding, with an abundant supply of catered food, cold cuts and cake and the harsh local "Stock" brandy. About half of the two hundred guests were white—many Polish-born friends and relatives of David's family. The other guests were black, Ethiopian-born Jews. Judith's sister, Ruth, had married in the same hall two years before, but mixed weddings like Judith's were rare. One Falasha veteran of the Israeli army, a member of a kibbutz near Tel Aviv, had married a *sabra*, whose Polish-born parents lived on the same kibbutz. The parents would have nothing to do with them. But the young wife, who became the mother of two mulatto children, felt that all of the other kibbutzniks had accepted them, and she expected that her parents would come around.

All the kibbutz Falashas were at the wedding, as well as the Falashas who worked at the port in Ashdod, or who were studying in technical schools or universities. There were also Yemenite Jews who had married Falasha girls they met when British forces liberated Ethiopia from the Italians in 1942 and who had brought their new wives to Palestine.

Judith missed her mother and father, and hoped they

would be allowed to come from Gondar to see her first child. She thought of them and of her brothers and sisters as she stepped under the *chupah*, the bridal canopy. A Sephardi rabbi performed the marriage ritual, the blessing and the reading of the *ketuba*, the marriage contract. At the end of the ceremony, a night of celebrating began in earnest . . .

JUDITH AND David moved to the Negev Desert development town of Arad, where she got a job as a cashier in the town's supermarket. David commuted to the nearby Dead Sea area, where he was employed as a metalworker, like his father. Occasionally they would go up to Herziliya to visit Judith's two brothers and her sister and cousins, and they would stop for a day or two in Ramat Gan so David's parents could dote on their grandson.

As the reports reached Israel of atrocities against the Falashas, Judith's anxiety grew. She and her brothers and sister had nightmares about the possible fate of their parents and their three remaining brothers and sisters in Gondar. "We think about them night and day," she told a friend. "We're constantly worrying about them. Things have gotten so bad and the response to our problem has been so little. The only solution is from God."

Israeli Exile

Rafi Tarfon's ex-wife, Rebecca, was married to him for thirty years. The American-born Israeli had been with Rafi during most of his years in Ethiopia. She was the one who persuaded him to leave Israel after he had been demoted from a top job in the development industry. Rebecca believed that he was the victim of politics, that he had lost his position because he wasn't a loyal Labor Party drone. Rafi also had an "authority problem," stemming from his service as an officer during the War of Independence. In the mid-1960s, they thought that it was time to leave Israel for a while. They decided on Ethiopia, where Israel's biggest aid-to-Africa effort was under way.

While Rafi served as an adviser to the Ethiopian government in Addis Ababa, Rebecca also worked. Their two daughters stayed in Israel, where they were attending college. In the course of his work, Rafi, a loner at heart, went on frequent trips into the countryside, leaving Rebecca alone in Addis, and she was miserable there. After four years in the country her eyesight had started to deteriorate, the consequence of one of Ethiopia's horrible eye diseases. She had come to think of Rafi as a fanatic who poured all of his love and energy into his work instead of his family, and they began to drift apart. She stayed with him for another three years, until finally, Rebecca felt she couldn't take it anymore. She left him just before the revolution, returning to Israel alone. But Rafi and his wife of so many years remained very close—he stayed with her during his leaves in Israel and called her frequently from Addis Ababa. Rebecca did her best to defend Rafi's efforts in Ethiopia against attacks by an opponent in Israel—attacks that had turned ugly and bitter. Rafi was finally forced out of his job—despite cries from the Falasha leaders, like Asa Azariah. "Rafi was removed because he was doing too good a job of organizing and working with the Falashas," Asa said bitterly. "No other Jew can just come in from England or the U.S. or Geneva and get along like that—he spent many years in Ethiopia, had the right connections—and he knew what he was doing. It's very hard to get close to our people. Very hard. But Rafi did it. There have been several emissaries sent out to the Falashas, but they come and go; none was as effective—they weren't taken into the community the way Rafi was. Most of the Falashas in Israel got letters from their families full of praise for Rafi. But he also made some enemies, and they dragged his name through the mud—a few Tigreans said he was no good and claimed he didn't get up to their villages. But it's not true. It just made it easier for ORT to get rid of him. He had so many solid programs going, he accomplished so much. Then they just pulled him out."

Rafi Tarfon stopped off in Israel on his way back to Ethiopia from Geneva, where he had been fired. He was returning to Addis Ababa to look for another job—in Ethiopia, Thailand, anywhere but Israel. It was August, 1977, a few weeks before sixty Falashas were flown to Israel in what was called a "breakthrough" in their long struggle to leave Ethiopia. Rafi, his whitened hair accented by white shorts and T-shirt, was jumpy and anxious to get back to Ethiopia, very uncertain about finding work and being able to stay there. He was even more guarded than usual about himself and the prospects for the Beta-Israel, although he told an Israeli Falasha that he believed the government was "really working on it now" and that a mass immigration to Israel was possible. But the aid effort to the Falashas was collapsing. "ORT is a disaster," he said. "They've destroyed everything that the Jewish aid groups have built up over the years."

Rafi looked tired and bent, his long involvement with Ethiopia about to end—he was a sixty-year-old maverick fired for insubordination, too old to get another job easily. The whole thing had broken his heart, Rebecca told friends, and she worried that Rafi was on the verge of suicide.

Less than three weeks after Rafi Tarfon went back to Addis Ababa to look for other work, Rebecca Tarfon heard the good news about the Beta-Israel and immediately called her daughter in Tel Aviv. "My friend in the Jewish Agency told me that sixty Falashas were flown in and that the operation was done with military precision," she said. She felt sure that Rafi helped plan it.

Reporter's Notes

I WAS SPENDING a few days in the towns of Upper Galilee waiting for permission to go to the immigrant camp near Tiberias. The story I had been following had taken a dramatic turn, and I was anxious to talk to some of the African Jews who had been secretly flown to Israel, especially the Falasha high priest, Aryeh Ben-David. On the sixth day after their arrival, I went to see them. The Falashas were being quartered in a Jewish limbo, an immigrant waystation in the north, where they had been taken directly after landing at a military base near the center of the country. Buses took them to the shores of Lake Kinneret—the Sea of Galilee—and up to an absorption center near the housing development that rises above Tiberias, one of the four holy cities of the Jews. Asking for directions to the immigrants' camp, I found that some Tiberians didn't even know that this ghost-town settlement still existed. It was filled to capacity a few years before, when thirty thousand Jews were arriving every year. But in September, 1977, it was virtually empty. On the other side of the barbed-wire fence surrounding the windswept center Arab shepherds led their black goats, which ravage the country's sparse shrubbery. It is desolate, thorny land—close to the big Galilee town yet in the middle of nowhere. A small number of Russians and other new immigrants were scattered among the identical pre-fab bungalows that are repeated in row after row. Three harried Israeli Absorption Ministry clerks were shuffling papers and slurping glasses of tea in the central office. The Falasha new arrivals, who had quadrupled the settlement's population, were met by several other Ethiopian Jews—veteran Israelis now, who would be helping their fellow tribesmen to join the mosaic of people that compose the Jewish state.

Black, bespectacled Noah Tefera wore an old-fashioned dark blue suit and tie in the gruelling September heat. He welcomed me in front of the absorption center office, shaking hands vigorously. Noah, a shy and serious man, had arrived in Israel in 1971 to become a *yeshiva bocher*, a religious student of the Talmud. After years of intensive study, he had become an ordained rabbi—the first in Beta-Israel history. Rabbi Tefera brimmed with joy over the arrival of the group of sixty, which included one of his sisters, for this group had been brought to Israel in what was expected to

become a new "magic carpet." Israeli planes had once trans-
ported many thousands of Yemenite Jews from southern
Arabia in Operation Magic Carpet. Perhaps it would also
happen to the Falashas. But it wasn't to be. Before the
clampdown on Falasha immigration caused by Moshe
Dayan's 1978 "slip of the tongue," only one more group of
another sixty Falashas would manage to follow the first
arrivals to Tiberias. The Ethiopians allowed both those
groups to leave under a "reunification of families" agreement with Jerusalem. Over the years, about one hundred
fifty other Falashas had managed to get into Israel, despite
the opposition of both Haile Selassie and the Israeli Labor
Party government (which in its last days had begun the
operation to bring the group of sixty.) When the first group
of Falashas was secretly allowed out—after epic changes of
government had occurred in both countries—the Beta-Israel
and their supporters were jubilant. The Ethiopian Jews were
being ransomed with guns. Noah Tefera was hoping that his
two brothers also would be joining him soon, for they had
just been released from detention.

Asa Azariah joined Noah and me as we headed toward
the bungalow of the high priest. Noah excitedly described
the big rescue effort that was supposed to continue in the
coming weeks. This was the vanguard, he said. The whole
tribe would be transplanted from Ethiopia to Israel.

The new arrivals, most of them still wearing their
traditional white *shamma* togas, had been in Israel for only
six days, and their culture shock was intense. Many had
never been outside their remote villages in the Ethiopian
highlands and couldn't imagine what magic would confront

them in Israel: exotic implements for cooking that use mysterious "gas"; water—hot or cold—from a pipe inside the house; glassy tile floors and windows in the walls—extraordinary for an Ethiopian peasant, whose mud dwelling has no opening other than a single door. Their deracination was far more complicated than that, for these backcountry villagers had been whisked away from feudalistic Ethiopian society and brought to earth in the middle of a modern, industrialized state.

"Village people are not used to having conveniences in the house, and they have to be taught things from scratch, all about the different food, how to wash a floor," Asa said as we passed an old woman and a toddler who were sweeping the area in front of a bungalow. "The gas is especially hard to explain—they just don't know how dangerous it is. They may leave it on all night, and we have to keep a constant check. Imagine how different it is just to get hot and cold water in your house. And the food is a very big problem too. No *teff* grows in Israel, so we are teaching them to make a local version of *injerra* out of wheat flour. It's just one of hundreds of things they have to get used to."

Another of the Israeli Falashas, Asfaw Toukaye, met us in the road. These three men were the leaders of the small Israeli Falasha community, and they had their hands full helping the newly arrived group to adjust to the immediate complexities of twentieth century life. But their biggest headache just then was the high priest of the Beta-Israel tribe, seventy-seven-year-old Aryeh Ben-David, whom I had come to see. Ben-David's admirers had said that he was among the greatest of holy men, "like unto Moses." His detractors said that he was the spirit of backwardness, a paranoid and a powerful troublemaker. Some of the Falashas engaged in the immigration effort thought that he was a major source of division in the community, an extreme egotist who had endangered the whole *aliyah* operation. Asfaw, a cousin of Ben-David's, said: "We had to bribe him, cajole him to leave Ethiopia before he ruined everything—that's the reason he's in this first group."

Hot, gusty *hamsin* winds swept dust off the brown hills encircling the absorption center. A group of African men scrutinized us from the terrace of Ben-David's bungalow, while their children played hopscotch in the tarmac road. The patriarch, clothed in a white robe and wielding a horsehair fly swatter like the kind used by Jomo Kenyatta, came out to greet us. Ben-David's male followers wore Western-style yarmulkes while he sported a black felt hat and looked every inch the African chief. "Elohim is great for giving us the sabbath," he said in Amharic as he pumped his guests' hands. Asfaw translated into Hebrew, often showing his impatience and dislike of the high priest.

Ben-David's deeply wrinkled face, dominated by clear, hazel-brown eyes and horsey yellow teeth, did not really convey the various characteristics attributed to him, and there was only a slight hint of the priest's intelligence. He seemed a vain but charming man, shifty, warm and humorous, with the polished manner of a veteran politican. And he possessed a treasury of his people's oral traditions and history, which he had learned from his father, also a *kes*, or priest. Ben-David sat surrounded by family as well as followers— his wife, three of his daughters, his son and several grandchildren had all arrived with him. The patriarch, a practiced storyteller holding court, cited a prophecy from

Isaiah to explain the events that were happening to his tribe, the Jews of Ethiopia. After the Exodus from Egypt, the Lord would "set his hand a second time," and this second Exodus would "recover the remnant of his people that shall remain from Assyria (Syria), and from Egypt, and from Pathos (Upper Egypt) and from Cush (Ethiopia) . . . And He will assemble the dispersed of Israel (the ten lost tribes) and gather together the scattered of Judah from the four corners of the earth."

The salvation of the Falashas was a "miracle," he said, and the House of Israel's rescue from Ethiopia was like Exodus. "When Moses told the Jews that he would free them from slavery, they didn't believe him," Ben-David said, "I feel it is the same now, the same as the miracle of Exodus." When I started to take notes Ben-David stopped me with his hand. "He asks you not to write in front of him," Asfaw said, "because it's the sabbath." Asfaw confided that *his* generation—Falashas in their twenties and thirties—didn't care about such things. But their fathers, men such as Aryeh Ben-David, were "like Naturei Karta," the fanatic sect of Hasidim living in Jerusalem. "My generation is totally removed from that—we're more assimilated," Asfaw said.

Ben-David's dramatic arrival in Israel a week before Rosh Hashana, the Jewish new year, had shaken him "like an earthquake." The high priest said he had always felt that his people existed in a vacuum. "There was something very basic missing from our lives in Ethiopia, a part of our spirit that wasn't there—it was the Holy Land. Thanks to God, what I had hoped for came true. The only thing I regret is that the whole community is not here yet. But they will come . . .

THE SIXTY FALASHAS numbered fifty-nine when they left Ethiopia—the last arrived two days later, traveling on his own. Aaron Yalo had lagged behind because he had been conscripted into the Ethiopian student "volunteer" corps and sent to a remote village hundreds of miles from Beta-Israel country. Aaron's two sisters and a brother had come to Israel several years before. Eleazar Yalo, who made his home in Rehovot, came to the Tiberias camp to see his brother. Tears of joy welled in the eyes of the two strikingly handsome young men as they were reunited after six years. Eleazar asked about the rest of the family in Gondar—his mother and father, and three other brothers and sisters.

The Yalos were joined in their bungalow by another pair of reunited brothers, Asa and Yonatan Azariah, and they all talked of reunion parties. The Yalo brothers planned a family gathering with their two sisters in Israel: Ruth, who was working as a nurse in Tel Aviv, and Judith Yalo-Bromberg, who was on a three-month maternity leave from her job as a supermarket clerk in the Negev town of Arad.

Asa Azariah and Eleazar Yalo also discussed the new list of names they were drawing up. "The list already includes two hundred fifty Beta-Israel, most of them students," Asa told me. "They will be brought next because their lives are in immediate danger."

Later, during a discussion about Israeli politics and its affect on the Beta-Israel, Eleazar proudly explained why he had voted for Begin's Likud Party. "I support their settlement policy, and we needed to get rid of the corrupt Labor Party people. The change was good for Israel—and for our tribe," he said. Asa, who had voted for Labor, agreed that in its first few months the new government was doing more for the Falashas than the Labor socialists had done in twenty-nine years. "Prime Minister Begin is a man of his word and I thank him from the bottom of my heart for helping our people. But I prefer Labor's stand on most issues, foreign and domestic."

As I left, Aaron and Eleazar Yalo extended an invitation to their forthcoming reunion and expressed the belief that family members left in Gondar would be joining them soon.

THE FALASHAS at Tiberias were supposed to be the first wave to reach Israel in the rescue of the tribe. Prime Minister Begin was reportedly "going all out" to save the Ethiopian Jews, saying in private meetings that "the Falasha community is one of the most ancient in the Jewish dispersion . . . and we must bring them home." And on Friday, August 25, 1977, the first group had been brought to Israel. The news media hadn't been informed, for the story was not to be published. Everyone understood the reason for the secrecy—premature publicity had torpedoed earlier efforts to bring Falashas to Israel. This was a life-or-death operation designed to preserve an endangered people.

But it was a fleeting moment of hope for the Falashas, as the Begin government proved to be as clumsy and basically indifferent to the fate of the lost tribe in Ethiopia as Labor had been. And Asa, Noah, Eleazar, Asfaw and the other Beta-Israel leaders would plunge from the euphoria of Tiberias in 1977 to the despair of 1979—the Jews of Israel, America and England were contributing to the liquidation of the Jews of Ethiopia, not to their salvation, they believed; and the promised miracle had turned into nothing more than a treacherous lie.

Epilogue

In November, 1979, the Israeli government, the Jewish Agency, and the World Zionist Organization announced the launching of a worldwide campaign to publicize the plight of the Falashas. Israel had changed tactics, reversing its policy of "quiet diplomacy." A cabinet minister, Moshe Nissim, told the Knesset: "We shall not rest in our efforts to secure for the Falashas the right to immigrate to Israel. Our Jewish brethren in Ethiopia are suffering from both physical and mental distress. The government is determined to enable them to come to live in Israel." And Radio Kol Israel announced that Prime Minister Begin had said: "We shall appeal to the Ethiopian government to let the Falashas go."

At the same time, the Falashas were reportedly becoming a major issue for the main American Jewish organizations—including B'nai B'rith, the American Jewish Congress, and the American Jewish Committee—which placed the Ethiopian Jews "at the top of the agenda." In a telegram to the National Jewish Community Relations Advisory Council, Begin claimed "We have done our utmost to bring them (the Falashas) to our historic homeland, Eretz Israel. . . . We are happy with the formation of the American committee to act on this great humanitarian issue with which our interdepartmental committee will cooperate."

But, according to *Maariv*'s Washington correspondent, Yuval Elitzur, even imaginative Israeli leaders like Ezer Weizman continued to say of the Falashas, "Tell me the truth—is this the most important issue we have to face now?" It was an echo of what Labor, Likud, and NRP officials had been saying all along—why bother about such

233

minor problems? Weizman told American Jewish students in December 1979 that the Falashas had not even been brought up in the Cabinet. He grew irritated with their questions, and finally dismissed the whole matter with his familiar wit: "Falashim Smalashim," he said. (The American students shared with other Falasha supporters a certain discomfort over the decision by Israel to make the Falashas a public campaign. They thought the announcement by Jewish Agency leaders was "cynical," an attempt to end the problem once and for all by arousing the anger of the Ethiopians.)

Elitzur's powerful article on the Falashas, which appeared in January 1980 claimed that the tribe's desperate situation and Israel's scandalous inaction over the years had had a profound impact on many prominent American Jews. "I'll tell you the truth," one wealthy contributor to Israel told him, "I won't spend money on Israel if Israel betrays its central obligation and trust—being a refuge for persecuted Jews." Elitzur, lamenting Israel's lack of candor about the issue, said Israeli officials don't understand why the subject is important to American Jews. "They brush it off by saying it's being taken care of." he told me. The correspondent, who felt certain that there was absolutely no color prejudice on the Israeli side, blamed the Jewish Agency for its inept handling of the whole affair.

The situation in Ethiopia was the same. Over a year after their arrest, the four Falasha religious teachers remained imprisoned. One of them was paralyzed from the waist down after being tortured. Another's leg had been smashed. Appeals for the release of these men went unheeded.

North American Jewish organization officials got the message firsthand when four Falasha leaders came to Montreal in November 1979 and told 2,000 representatives of Jewish federation groups that the Jewish Agency, ORT, and some Israeli officials had obstructed the rescue of the Beta-Israel tribe. "Our final hour is near," a Falasha elder told the overflow audience, "Until when shall we cry?"

The major Jewish organization in the United States and Canada started to take up the Falasha cause and to apply pressure on the Israeli government; and by spring, 1980, the Jewish Agency began to get some results, in operations that could not be publicized. But some Falasha leaders remained pessimistic, saying that these positive actions were too little too late. There was no doubt that something was in the wind: Prime Minister Begin announced to a women's group that an endangered Jewish community would soon be brought to Israel. Although that could mean Syrian Jews or Iranian or Turkish Jews, most observers believed that the remnant of the Beta-Israel tribe would be saved.

Selected Bibliography

A. d'Abbadie "Rapport sur les Falachas" *Archives Israelite*, 1846.

Adler, Cyrus "Bibliography of the Falashas" *The American Hebrew*, 1894, (16/111).

Adler, E. N. *Jewish Travelers*, New York, 1930.

Aescoly, A. Z. "The Falashas: A Bibliography" *Kiryat Sepher*, XII: 254-65, 370-83, 498-505. XIII: 250-65, 383-93, 506; 1935-7.
   Sefer Hafalashim, Jerusalem, 1943.

Beckingham, C. F. and G. W. B. Huntingford *Some Records of Ethiopia 1593-1646*, London, 1954.

Brecher, Michael *The Foreign Policy System of Israel*, London, 1972.

Bruce, James *Travels to Discover the Source of the Nile*, Edinburgh (5 vols), 1804.

Budge, E. A. *A History of Ethiopia, Nubia & Abyssinia*, London, 1928.

Cheeseman, R. E. *Lake Tana and the Blue Nile*, London, 1936.

Cline, W. *Mining and Metallurgy in Negro Africa*, Paris, 1937.

Conti Rossini "Appunti di storia e letteratura Falascia" *Rivista degli studi orientali*, Rome, 1920 pp. 563–610.
   Storia d'Etiopia, Rome, 1928.

Dubois, W. E. B. *The World and Africa*, New York, 1946.

Faitlovitch, J. "The Falashas" *American Jewish Yearbook* 5681, 22: pp. 80-110, Philadelphia, 1920.
   Voyage to the Falashas (in Hebrew), Tel Aviv, 1959.

Flad, J. M. *The Falasha (Jews) of Abyssinia*, London, 1869.
   A Short Description of the Falashas and Kamants, London, 1866.

Forbes, R. J. *Metallurgy in Antiquity*, London, 1950.

Freehof, S. B. "Marriage with Falashas" *A Treasury of Responsa*, Philadelphia, pp. 122-127.

Ginsburg, Louis *Legends of the Jews, 1909–1913, Philadelphia*

Gobat, Samuel *Journal of Three Years' Residence in Abyssinia*, London, 1834.

Godbey, A. H. *The Lost Tribes: A Myth*, New York, 1930.

Goiten, E. D. "Note on Eldad the Danite" *Jewish Quarterly Review*, Vol. XVII 1926-27.

Gordon, Cyrus *The Ancient Near East*, New York, 1965.

Halevy, J. *La Guerre de Sarsa Dengil. Travels in Abyssinia*, London, 1877.

Harris, W. *The Highlands of Aethiopia*, London, 1844.

Hess, R. L. "An Outline of Falasha History" *Proceedings of the Third International Conference of Ethiopian Studies* (Institute of Ethiopian Studies), Addis Ababa, pp. 99-112.

    "Toward a History of the Falasha" *East African History*, McCall, Bennet & Bulter, eds, New York, 1969.

Huntingford, G. W. B. *Some Records of Ethiopia, 1593-1646, The Glorious Victories of Amda Seyon*, Oxford, 1969.

Leslau, Wolf *Falasha Anthology*, New York, 1951.

    Coutumes et Croyances des Falachas, Paris, 1957.

    "A Falasha Religious Dispute" *Proceedings of the American Academy for Jewish Research* XVI, pp. 71-95, 1947.

    "A Supplementary Falasha Bibliography" *Studies in Bibliography and Booklore*, II pp. 9-27, 1957.

    "To the Defense of the Falashas" *Judaism* v.2, 1957.

Luzzato, P. "Memoire sur les Juifs d'Abyssinie" *Archives Israelities*, v. 12-15, Paris, 1851-54.

Markakis, J. *Ethiopia: Anatomy of a Traditional Polity*, London, 1974.

Messing, Simon "Journey to the Falashas" *Commentary*, XXII, 1956.

Norden, Herman *Africa's Last Empire*, London, 1930.

Payne, E. *Ethiopian Jews: The Story of a Mission*, London, 1972.

Pearce, N. *Life and Adventures*, London, 1831.

Pritchard, James *Solomon and Sheba*, London, 1974.

Quirin, J. *The Beta Israel (Felasha) in Ethiopian History*, Dissertation, University of Michigan, 1977.

Rathjens, C. *Die Juden in Abessinien*, Hamburg, 1921.

Sachar, Howard *A History of Israel*, New York, 1976.

Schoenberger, Michelle *The Falashas of Ethiopia: An Ethnographic Study*, Dissertation, University of Cambridge, 1975.

Schoff, W. *The Periplus of the Erythryan Sea*, London, 1912.

Sergew Hable Sellassie *Ancient and Medieval Ethiopian History to 1270*, Addis Ababa, 1972.

Shelemay, K. *The Liturgical Music of the Falashas of Ethiopia*, Dissertation, University of Michigan, 1977.

Simoons, F. *Northwest Ethiopia: Peoples and Economy*, Madison, Wisc., 1960.

    "The Agricultural Implements and Cutting tools of Begemder and

Semyon" *Southwestern Journal of Anthropology,* v. 14 pp. 386-406, 1958.

Stern, H. *Wanderings Among the Falashas,* London, reprinted 1968.

Taddesse Tamrat *Church and State in Ethiopia 1270-1527,* Oxford, 1972.

Trimingham, J. S. *Islam in Ethiopia,* London, 1952.

Ullendorff, E. *The Ethiopians,* Oxford, 1960.

  Ethiopia and the Bible, Oxford, 1967.

Wurmbrand, Max "Fragments d'anciens escrits Juifs dans la litterature Falacha" *Journal Asiatique,* 1954, pp. 83-100.

  "The Falashas," Encyclopedia Judaica.

Glossary

ETHIOPIAN WORDS

abba—priest
ambda—mountain, rock
ayhud—Jew
baria—see *shangalla*
birr—Ethiopian dollar
buda—possessor of evil eye, devil
habasha—Ethiopia
injerra—Ethiopian bread
kayla—see *buda*
kes—priest
kita—unleavened bread
orev—Noah's raven
orit—the Torah
seyon—Zion, the Ark
shamma—toga, white robes
shangalla—slave
shifta—bandit
tabiban—smith tribe
tabot—replica of the Ark
tayb—smith
teff—Ethiopian grain
tekel, or *tukul*—hut
wot—sauce
zar—spirit

HEBREW WORDS

aliyah—ascent to Israel
aliyah beth—Jewish immigration to
    Palestine
Beta-Israel—House of Israel
charash—smith, magic
chupah—bridal canopy
chutzpah—brazenness, impudence
cohen(im)—priest(s)
cushi—black
etrog—citron
gaonim—wise men
g'dolim—important sages
goy(im)—gentile(s)
hadani—the Danite
habash—Ethiopia
halacha—Jewish Law
kain—metal weapon
kashrut—kosher laws
ketuba—marriage contract
mikva—ritual bath
mitzva—commandment, duty
mumzerim—bastards
nappeh—user of bellows
sabra—native Israeli
schvartzes—(Yiddish) blacks
shaliach—envoy
ulpan—Hebrew school
yeshiva(ot)—religious school(s)
yeshiva bocher—religious student

Index

243